Identifying & Healing From Narcissistic Abuse So You Can Thrive

SHAYNE N. EDSON

ISBN: 1986455599
ISBN-13: 978-1986455596

DEDICATION

This book is dedicated to all you beautiful souls in this world who deserve better. Who always have. To all whose good hearts were used against them by those with no qualms whatsoever. By those without conscience. By those who are entirely soulless. It's time you healed.

CONTENTS

ACKNOWLEDGMENTS

I acknowledge the priceless help in my own personal journey to be able to identify and heal from narcissistic abuse so that I could thrive from the following people:
Lisa A. Romano
Margaret Paul
Ross Rosenberg
Jerry Wise
Whom I remain unspeakably indebted to indefinitely. These people I credit to having helped me more than any others. The work that they do is amazing and far reaching.

INTRODUCTION

What qualifies me as an author to write about this subject? I spent the first approximately forty years of my life in a nightmare of sorts. There were so many things about myself and my behaviour that puzzled me. There was so much in my own biological "family" that felt wrong. It simply didn't feel safe. It simply didn't feel like love. There was seemingly so much that simply didn't seem to make sense. Or if it did, I couldn't make any sense of it. I was bewildered. I was confused. I had depression. I had complex PTSD. I had a mental fog. I had no self worth or self esteem. And yet, I wanted to be the best that I could be. Goodness knows, I desperately tried.

When I turned forty, I simply had to write my childhood autobiography, "Surviving Childhood". (Available on Payhip.com) Which drained me emotionally. What I realise now is that the problem was I never actually had a sense of self. I was actually so enmeshed with my biological family members. They used guilt, manipulation, blame, shame, and whatever else worked to get me to do what they wanted. It didn't matter if underneath it all I begrudgingly didn't want to do it, I just did. It seemed as if I couldn't say no.

Why was it that I almost committed suicide at the age of thirty three? Why was it that I was on antidepressants for almost nine years? Why was it that the thought of going off antidepressants scared me? And felt like it was to be avoided at all costs? Why was it that even on antidepressants, I had occasions where I felt suicidal? Why did I cry in bed and just want to die? Why, why, why? Why did I seemingly not have any control over how I acted? Why did I have outbursts of anger and wonder where they came from? Why did I eat junk, and not look after myself? Why couldn't I seem to get on with my life?

Why was it that it felt like I was always giving, yet I resented it? Shouldn't giving feel good? Why was it that I thought that the only way I could get any kind of "love" was based on what I did? Why did I not trust most people? Why was it that I rarely had any close friendships? Why were my parents and some siblings so hypocritical, self righteous, and pious? Why, quite frankly, were they horrible people? And why were they horrible to me? Why did I seem to push my wife away? Why was it I seemed to even push my daughter away? Why when I wanted to simply be a good person did it seem to be so difficult?

And so, enough was enough. I'd had enough pain. I began looking for answers. I even tried helping others do the same through social media. However, I got too overwhelmed. I still absorbed other people's pain far too much. And I couldn't handle it. I had to leave the group I'd created to help others, and give it to someone else to take over. And fast. You see, whilst I had learned a little, I had had no change on an inner level.

And so I began to look for more answers. And I found them. I devoured them. I was finally able to understand myself. I was finally understanding why my parents and my older siblings were the way that they were. I not only identified the kind of abuse that had hindered me for all of my life up until that point was termed as narcissistic, but I was able to heal from the inner wounding it had caused me at such a young age, and that had stayed with me well into my adult years.

I now began to thrive. I was in the best place of my entire life, and there was no going back. And so, as I had wanted to do, I knew that I simply must share what I had discovered with others. How many more people had lived their lives similarly to myself, whilst also not having yet solved the puzzle? I realised that a lot of psychologists would actually do more harm than good with those who have been victims of this kind of abuse. Why? Because, they have no understanding of this type of abuse. Nor necessarily the effect and feelings on the part of the victims. This means that many people could be retraumatised, and/or retriggered by going to such psychologists. Quite frankly, the last thing they needed. And so, the need for this book to be written.

The best teacher in life is experience, it is said. When it comes to narcissistic abuse, this is definitely the case. The only way to know what it's like, is to have been there. To have walked in the same shoes. Yes, there can be physical and sexual abuse related to the narcissistic abuse. However, it can also be solely psychological and emotional abuse. Never let anyone pooh pooh this away, as if of little consequence.

You see, narcissistic people are shrewd at concealing their abuse. Much abuse is only done in private, behind closed doors, as it were. Financially, a narcissist can drain their victims. And in other ways too. A person can have their inner self eaten away at, eroded so much to the extent that they are crippled, in effect. With a narcissist, they use all kinds of strategies and techniques to manipulate their victims. Whatever will keep them under their control. It's insidious. Pure and simple.

Victims need to have their voice heard. Narcissists are so good at changing their persona to whatever fits their agenda to get their vile, selfish needs met at any given time that people wouldn't know at once that the person is a narcissist. They can be high functioning. They've mastered the art of deception.

On a final note, I'm here to support all narcissistic victims. However, whilst I am here to support them, the inner work can only be done by each individual person. No one could do it for me but me. No one can do it for them but them. May this book help all who have been victims of narcissistic abuse to not only identify, and to heal from this kind of abuse, but to thrive to the point where they move on with life. And be the best that they can be. Free from any parasitic narcissists previously in their lives.

1

WHAT'S A NARCISSIST?

You tried to explain the behaviour away. You always did. And they gladly had you feeling that it was you. Never them. It was always you hadn't done this, or you hadn't done that. You were responsible. How could you be such a repugnant human being? So abominable? Yet, you're actually far from it. You're anything but like how they either made you feel, outrightly said you were, or implied. You are a good person. No, not perfect. But, overall, a good person. You're honest. You're kind. You're empathetic. You'd give the shirt off your own back to whoever needed it. Right? How do I know this? Because, I, dear friend, was a lot like you. In fact, to a degree, I still am.

That being said, now something's occurred to you. It's hit you. Like a freight train at full speed perhaps. In essence, that something is this: You woke up to the reality of the difference between what was said, and what was done. Finally, you either began or are right now beginning to seek answers. Because, let's be brutally honest with each other right here, right now: It has simply never felt right.

That feeling in your gut? It can no longer be ignored, can it? Suddenly, you realise that something doesn't match up. The actions simply do not correspond to the words. Actually, upon reflection, it's always been that way, hasn't it? My dear friend, you can no longer ignore the memory stick, can you? Why? Because enough is enough. You've had enough pain. And you know somehow that this person, or persons have caused this.

It doesn't matter what you do, it's never enough. And this person, or persons, leave you feeling drained. Depleted. Like your tank is literally empty. Emotionally. It's as if you've given your all, until there's nothing left. Which is likely because you have. They've drained you. Spiritually, emotionally, mentally, physically. Why?

Because, and this might hit you right in the eye sockets as if with a hammer proverbially speaking: they are a narcissist. They were take, take, take with you, and you were give, give, give with them: am I right? And here is why. Unknowingly, you were reactive to an insidious, horrid "game" they've been playing with you. Perhaps for days, perhaps for months, perhaps for years, maybe even for decades. You were giving them what is referred to as narcissistic supply. Which I'll talk about in more detail later on in this book.

Here's what it's vitally important that you accept the reality of: It doesn't matter what the relationship is between them and you: they could be a sibling, parent, co worker, boss, spouse or partner, a "friend", a religious minister even: they simply have what is known as
narcissistic personality disorder (NPD). Long story short, you've been dealing with an emotional toddler with an ego that needed you, and whoever else provided it to prop it up. And this is a fact: they feed (or fed) off your pain.

What that means is this: your feelings don't matter. If you didn't realise before, they never have. They cannot feel empathy for you. They are masters of justification. So don't expect a genuine apology. Nor any admission of accountability. You are dealing with someone who hates you. Yes, hates you. They hate everybody. They hate themselves.

They project onto you. For example, what they accuse you of, it's actually likely an admission about themselves. How they feel about themselves. They actually feel like a failure. They target people who have things that they want. They have a very unstable identity. You are supposed to hide anything you might be good at, so that they can shine.

They are guided by emotion. Not logic, not intelligence. As an example: if you're smiling, you must be laughing at them. Keep this in mind, because any attempt to explain your motive, well, let's just say this: save your breath. Explaining is useless. Futile.

Do they have a sense of entitlement? If so, tick off another box. Basically, a combination of neglect and being spoilt has created this disorder. Yes, you are dealing with a disordered person. The patterns of thinking they developed in their earliest years was a way for their brain to cope. The only thing is they're now in an adult body. But you are dealing with someone whose emotions never developed. An emotionally stunted individual. A two to four year old, despite what age they actually are. This is why no logic, no reasoning matters. The patterns of thinking are so deeply entrenched, that whatever they feel is, (at least in their view) fact. They create chaos and torment to get attention. So all you are to them is a means to this sadistic end.

An important point to keep in mind is this: At some point, most likely before the age of five years of age, a conscious choice was made by the narcissist or narcissists in your life to squish out any empathy. Let that sink in. So, in their view: It's them against the world. Against you. Against everyone.

This is, of course, part of their polarised thinking.

Whereas an emotionally more healthy person can see that it isn't always black or white, one way or another. A more healthy emotionally person sees that there are often varying degrees of in between. Not a narcissist, though. They can't. They won't.

And whilst they are the very source of their own pain, it'll always be someone else blamed. "They/You made me do it." There's always a justification of one kind or another: At least, to them. In their view. Which, by the way, is the only one that matters.

Any vulnerability must be avoided at all costs. For a narcissist, they must never show any vulnerability. Or humility. And, for the record, there's no chance of their emotions being anything but fake. They morph to take on whatever persona they feel is needed at any given time to get what they need. A narcissist can't truly feel love. A narcissist can't feel empathy. Basically, you are dealing with an inhuman beast. Who will alternate between playing one of two things: either the hero, or the victim/martyr.

At this point, I am going to share personal instances in this regard. You see, my biological mother, along with the sibling closest to me in age, (although he's seven years my senior) are both narcissists. They both have narcissistic personality disorder. In my brother's case, I dare say our biological parents are the reason. I'm also aware that in my mother's case, she supposedly had a less than desirable family upbringing in her earliest years.

On at least one occasion during my earliest years that I can recall, my mother and brother intervened, in effect saving my life. When I was five, walking home from school, I had a knife held to my throat by an older boy. As this happened, my mother appeared from around the corner. When I was about seven, I went under the water, and would have drowned in a backyard pool whilst we were visiting some people. My brother was in the pool, and although I can remember a lot of water coming out of my body afterwards, he did get me out of the pool. His mate was there, too. The point I am getting at is that in both instances they could be seen to be the hero. It had nothing whatsoever to do with feeling anything for me in the way of empathy. In fact, after the actual event, I don't recall anything from either of them. There was no comfort. No anything.

Have you ever watched the BBC show, "Keeping Up Appearances"? If so, you will understand that the character the entire show is based around is a narcissist: Hyacinth Bucket. And when you watch it knowing that, you'll see what happens in an entirely different light than previously. In fact, now that I'm aware of it, I'm not sure I could watch it ever again.

If you haven't watched the show, I suggest you look it up online, and do so. You will see this when you do, in each and every episode: Hyacinth has no empathy whatsoever. It's always all about her. Getting what she wants. Getting what she needs. However she can. It's about her keeping up appearances, exactly like the title. Propping up that narcissistic "false self", the pretend, fabricated "wonderful" person the narcissist loves to present themselves to the world as. There's always an agenda. It's relentless.

You'll also notice that Hyacinth couldn't care less about her "less fortunate" sisters, Daisy and Rose. Let alone

Daisy's husband, Onslow. So much so that she hides them, along with any evidence they are around, if at all possible. On the other hand, Hyacinth repeatedly mentions her wealthy sister Violet, and brags of her wealth, whenever able to. Along with her own son, Sheridan, who is at University. Interestingly, Sheridan never seems to want to come home and visit his mother, Hyacinth. In essence: If you want to see a show that highlights the dynamics of relationships in regards to a narcissist, this one is must see viewing.

Not to mention the trail of disaster Hyacinth inevitably leaves behind, in her wake. Just like narcissists do. Because they don't care for consequences. They don't care for anyone else. It's simply something they're unable to do.

A narcissist is a hypocrite. They simply are the epitome of hypocrisy. If you ever do, (and I speak from experience), attempt to point this out to them, and/or call them out on it, you will incur what's known as "narcissistic rage". And whilst they can dish it out to you, there's no way they can take it. For real. Actually, when I called my mother out years ago on her hypocrisy, she got my enabling father, her husband, to reply by letter to my letter. And nothing was resolved. In fact, all that happened was mean and hurtful things were flung and expressed at my expense.

Take note: In the instance of a couple who stay together for many years, when one is the narcissist, it's not a normal, healthy relationship. And, as was so with my father, he'd throw myself or any other of his own offspring at the proverbial altar of my narcissistic mother, so that he avoided being the recipient of her narcissistic rage. He is what's referred to as an enabling spouse. Not once did he ever stand up for me. As would be the same for his other older five children preceding me.

Here's an example from my own narcissistic mother regarding what's called projection: She said some years ago that if I was going to be nasty, she didn't want me to come and stay there. Me. I was the nasty one. Guess who actually is the nasty one? Yep. You guessed it. Her.

You see, all a narcissist can do inevitably is to push people away. And if you are the truthteller in the family, like myself, the one who calls it how it is, whilst the rest say nothing, or participate as contributors in this dysfunctional mess, you'll become the "scapegoat". It's messed up, but it is what it is, my dear friend.

Here's what's critical that you must always remember: No normal rules apply with narcissists. None whatsoever. And invalidation of your feelings, of your emotions, of your experience, of your truth: they specialise in that. And when you remember something, anything that doesn't portray them in the best light, that "false self" fabricated one, they'll make out as if it never happened. That it's a figment of your imagination. Don't be fooled by that, though, my dear friend. Trust your memories. Why? Simply put, because your memories do not lie. What you remember is spot on.

As for being seen as a separate person, with free will: not a chance. A narcissist sees you as their property, an extension of them. Do not expect to be seen as anything other than that, or you will set yourself up for being retraumatised and/or reabused by them.

This, in my personal instance, actually was liberating. Once I realised this, a lot more made sense. Along with how they'll twist and distort words, sentiments, and so on to get whatever is on their agenda to get. You'll also set yourself up for retraumatisation and/or reabuse when you fall for this, too. You see, they're experts at what they do. And their ego must be paramount above all else. Consequences and cost is of no matter to them.

You may or may not have suffered physical and/or sexual abuse at the hands of the narcissist or narcissists in your life. It may be emotional and psychological abuse you have suffered, without the other types of abuse initially mentioned. Whatever the case in your personal instance, do not permit anyone to minimise the abuse you have suffered at the hands of this person or persons.

Furthermore, many people won't understand what you've been through, nor how it has affected you. Even though this may be so, the kind of abuse you have suffered has been compared to that of being a prisoner of war. A war that you never asked for, at that.

Once you've identified what you've been through, you might wish to tell people. Even during the healing process, which is best done away from the narcissist or narcissists in your life, if at all possible, you might want to do this. However, before you do, please bear this in mind: You need to be extremely selective about who you talk about this with, and/or communicate it with in other ways. Are they in contact with the narcissist or narcissists in your life? If there's a chance they even might be, it would be best to not disclose this information to these people.

I say this to you because I care. I also mention it due to the fact that I found out the hard way from personal experience that you can feel hurt when someone you confided in about what you've been through, how it's affected you for much of your life, how it's damaged you for so long, held you back, and so on reacts. I experienced reactions from people to the effect of they clammed up, they did not respond at all, be it in person verbally, or via text message or other forms of communication.

Which helped me see who my real friends were. After I had pondered to myself: Why weren't these people happy that the lights had gone on, that I'd figured this out, that I'd even gotten off antidepressants, which I'd been on for almost nine years? Why weren't they happy that I would no longer be abused, that I wouldn't allow it ever again? Some reactions seemed to be along the lines of that I shouldn't have said anything about it, as if it was of little or no consequence, as if they genuinely didn't care. All part of a learning process for me in which I came out more discerning.

That being said, on the positive, you have access to a vast number of people who've been through similar to what you've been through: online. And these people are massively supportive, compassionate and understanding.

I have found Twitter and Instagram to be better than FaceBook in this regard. FaceBook can be overwhelming is why I say this. If you get into a large group on there, with the concept of support, it can tend to get out of hand. Also, it does seem as if people can be somewhat triggered in such an atmosphere. Overstimulation isn't good for you. In my experience, FaceBook is the site for overstimulation. And I was on there for quite a few years. To be honest, I didn't get Twitter initially, but now I do, and I enjoy it immensely. As for Instagram, surprisingly, it has become my favourite. Through both my Twitter and Instagram accounts I've connected with so many truly beautiful and amazing people.

If in your experience, as was the case in mine, you experienced so much narcissistic abuse that it's all that you can remember, please be aware that this abuse has shaped you. You will likely have a mind filled with negativity, critical of yourself, and also others. What this also likely means is that you may have some narcissistic traits. However, please realise this doesn't mean you are a narcissist. Nor does it mean that you have a personality disorder. The very fact that you are reading this speaks volumes that you do not. Why can I say this with so much confidence? Simply because people who have narcissistic personality disorder have no self reflection. Whereas you do. Or else you wouldn't be here, looking for some answers, looking to find out why you have been in such a world of pain. Possibly for all of your life.

Here is the good news: Part of the healing process will get this junk out of you. I'm excited for you, because I know you are going to feel lighter than you may ever have in your entire life. And whilst you mightn't realise it yet, you only have it there in the first instance because of the dysfunctional programming full of negative messages you absorbed in your earliest years. Here's one more thing: Our brains can be rewired, in effect. Which means you have the ability to change all that rubbish that's held you back for so long, and it's easier than you may think.

Like myself, perhaps you have had depression for a long time. I'm thrilled to let you know that once you understand and get to the root cause of this, it's actually easily fixed. In the meantime, my dear friend, please be assured of this: Depression is a normal response to adverse conditions. Covert or overt abuse of any kind, narcissistic included, absolutely is classed as adverse conditions.

When all you may have absorbed and been told was basically of a negative nature from someone or ones who supposedly love you, who supposedly are meant to be your nearest and dearest, who invalidated your feelings, making you feel invisible in effect, also that your feelings didn't matter, how else could you feel? You simply had to push those feelings down, i.e. depress them. And, you also might have had to stay in your head, as it were. I certainly did. To escape mentally from the constant barrage of psychological abuse you were powerless to escape from at that time.

In my instance, I loved reading. Books were my escape. Also, at times, depending on where we lived, I was fortunate enough to have either a bush reserve at my disposal after simply going over the backyard fence, or to live out of town in the country. Meaning I could also just go for a walk, spend however much time I wished to: so I could simply be. Basically, it felt better to simply be away from my dysfunctional family members. To escape, even if unable to do so more than temporarily at that time.

Of course, I realise your situation may be different.

Please, dear friend, whatever your situation is, do not at this crucial point give up finding out more about the kind of abuse you have and may be continuing to suffer from, nor how you can, in effect, break free from this abuse, and/or your abuser. I tell you, dear friend, it is worth it. You are worth it. And, yes, that's likely something you're not used to hearing, but it's true. Please feel free to repeat it to yourself, either in your mind, or out loud when alone. Daily. As many times as you can do so. Why? Because right now, you need to realise that you are so very worth it. That you are so very much more than the abuse you have suffered or are suffering from still. That it's actually because you are that is partly why you've become the narcissist or narcissists in your life's emotional punching bag. And that an utterly empty, miserable being/s want you to be as miserable as they are.

2

INSIGHTS ABOUT THE NARCISSIST

"They love me. In their own way." So the rationalising goes. Simply because the narcissist or narcissists in your life have most likely trained you to think that. Brainwashed you even. From time to time, they seem sweet. They seem to say nice things to you. Am I right? I know I am. I know because I was under this delusion, this fantasy about my biological mother for most of my life.

But you know what? The actions always contradicted the words. This alternation between sweetness and meanness with the narcissist or narcissists in your life is a trick they use to suck you back in so they can abuse you all over again. In fact, that supposed "niceness" on their part, a fake declaration of their "love", it's even been given the term "hoovering".

I'll give you an example regarding the actions not matching up with the words: In my entire school life, my narcissistic personality disordered biological mother never went to the school for anything other than what gave her a chance to portray herself as the hero. I literally can count on one hand how many times that was. In over ten years of schooling.

In fact, it was actually only three times. Three instances. The first one related to the knife at my throat incident I mentioned in the last chapter. The second was in the last year of primary school when some girls in my class had a bit of fun with me, telling innocent me to ask my mother what tampons were. Which I did. So, that was the second instance. She went up to be the "hero" by talking to my teacher, in typical narcissistic style, so she could lord it over them. Lastly, the next year, which was my first year of High School. After I'd been bullied by a couple of boys to the point that I punched one in the face. He was a couple of years older than me. Also, bigger. However, I'd taken enough rubbish from him, so one day, I snapped. Hence, the punch. Long story short, I can't even remember how she found out, but she did, and went up to see the school principal about it. Not once did she go to the school to see me do anything. Not once did she go to the school to participate in anything. Even my enabling father did go once. To watch me perform in my final year of high school. Then, said nothing, and acted as if it hadn't happened. Heaven forbid I have any kind of creativity, let alone that it be acknowledged that I was good at anything.

Let this sink in properly: Loyalty is the highest virtue taught by abusers and used as a control tool. Once again, twisted and distorted by them to their benefit. Not yours. And the play the old "family" card if it's a relative abusing you, equals priceless arsenal for them.

Crazymaking is another of a narcissists specialties. By making you appear crazy, they come off looking better. When what's actually happening is you are responding to an injustice on their part, to a lack of any kind of responsibility or accountability. Don't expect them to ever do anything other than avoid, skirt around, change the topic, or some other diversion strategy/technique that takes the heat off of them.

Which is precisely the reason why I said in the previous chapter to trust your memories. Yes, the narcissist will crazymake in regards to them. They'll try and make out it never happened. Because by doing so, they avoid facing up to anything that paints them in less than the very best light. Narcissists are experts when it comes to avoidance. And they'll do it so smoothly, you'll question your own mind.

My narcissistic personality disordered older brother spent a lot of time with a girl when he was in the first year or two of high school. To be honest, the girl in question was not attractive, was rather loud from what I recall, and had funny teeth. Now, all I did once some years ago was mention her name, and he reacted as if I was crazy. Why do you think? Because how would it have made him look? To be seen as the actual desperate loser that he was/is, right? Bingo.

Simply put, there's no way a narcissist could keep anyone in a relationship with them if they didn't use all of the strategies that they do. Why else would people go back over and over again to put up with the rubbish they dish out? Now, that being said, I mean no disrespect to you whatsoever. So please don't take it that way. Truly. Because, I too was "stuck" in the abuse cycle like you have been, or may still be, dear friend.

And it's because we are at heart, such beautiful people. Beautiful souls. It really is. The thing is, we've been trampled over for likely such a long time, we accepted it. Do you realise why we did? Because we didn't see it for the abuse that it was. I mean to say, it didn't feel right, did it? Something felt wrong. However, we were, or in your case, likely are still, what's referred to as a codependent. Codependency has kept you trapped, as it kept me trapped previously.

So what's this all about, I hear you asking. This codependency. Being codependent. Here is an online definition of codependency: excessive emotional or psychological reliance on a partner, typically one with an illness or addiction who requires support. It's also referred to as trauma addiction.

Basically, the kind of person you are, the kind of person I am, is the opposite in effect to the kind of person that a narcissist is. We continued to vainly and futilely attempt to win the love of a narcissist or narcissists. Whereas you and I are such giving people, narcissists are simply takers. But let me guess, because I know I felt this way: You feel you're lovable only to the extent you care for others. To use a term that might be new to you, but meant the world to me: you are in a state of self love deficit disorder. I was too.

In my case, I was raised by authoritarian parents. Yes, my biological mother is narcissistic personality disordered. However, my father was her willing accomplice. He was her enabler. And he did whatever to avoid being the target of her narcissistic rage. They were, in effect, partners in crime. Now, authoritarian parenting is parenting that expects a child to act like an adult. And you are robbed of any kind of childhood. It's also basically a "Do as we say, not as we do" type of parenting. It's messed up. Is it any wonder then that we have so many beautiful people all around this planet who end up as adults with the accompanying effects of feelings of worthlessness, no self esteem, no self love? And when I refer to self love, I am talking about the healthy kind, not the egotistical garden variety. The narcissistic kind.

So, for me, I was conditioned by my biological parents that any "love" from them was conditional. I had to be on my best behaviour. That kind of "You must be perfect to be loved" thinking. It's ludicrous, I know. But, when you don't realise why you are the way you are, how used you have been by these people, you continue in the same cycle. Nothing changes. Until that beautiful day when you finally wake up.

And, for the record, of course I couldn't get the love of authoritarian parents. Both of whom had no self love. This is huge, but here goes: How can they love you when they don't even love themselves? Think about the narcissist or narcissists in your life, whoever they are, my dear friend. Because the same rules apply to them. At this point, I could let go of the fantasy that my mother would ever love me, that my father too would ever love me, in an emotionally connected way.

This is when it should hit you as it did me like a lightning bolt: It was never our fault. It's never been our fault. We all came into this world as a beautiful, lovable little one. Whatever caused the narcissist or narcissists in your life to become narcissists has never had anything to do with us.

However, we were taught to be people pleasers, that we had to gain approval/validation from others, outside of ourselves. (More brainwashing) This keeps us captive prisoners to the narcissist or narcissists in our lives. And their accomplices, too. And believe me, as messed up as it is, they do have accomplices. More than one.

At this point, I suggest to you that it may well be to your benefit as it was mine to view the videos available on YouTube by Lisa A. Romano, Dr Margaret Paul, Ross Rosenberg, and Jerry Wise. Yes, there are other people who you might benefit from listening to also, but these people are the ones who resonated most with me, and who I credit with my understanding and healing to the point of healthy self love, to the point of now having gone and maintained "no contact" with basically all members of my biological family. Who, let's face it, have done absolutely nothing or next to nothing for me.

Please bear in mind these four people have been through what you and I have been through, my dear friend. They have an amazing understanding, coupled with real feeling and compassion to share what they have learned with others. Do not go to a therapist. Do not. Why? Because, you could be set backwards. And if you take the narcissist or narcissists in your life along, the therapist could well end up taking their side. Basically, you are most likely opening yourself up to not heal, to be traumatised over and over again, and spend a lot of wasted time and money in the process. And no, I'm not kidding.

Remember, this is a person who can ooze charm when it suits their agenda. Then turn like that. A person who makes you seem like the crazy one. A person who uses secrecy as a tool. A person who is so sneaky. A person who uses what's termed triangulation. Not that they care about any of those people whom they have triangulated, in the process. Basically, you are dealing with a snake in the grass.

Now, a little more about triangulation. Here's an online definition of it: A manipulation tactic where one person will not communicate directly with another person, instead using a third person to relay communication to the second, thus forming a triangle. It is also a form of splitting in which one person manipulates a relationship between two parties by controlling communication between them. Triangulation may manifest itself as a manipulative device to engineer rivalry between two people, known as divide and conquer or playing one (person) against another.

So, the narcissist in your life might be badmouthing you to someone else, whilst simultaneously badmouthing them to you. And be telling both of you to keep it a secret. To keep it to yourselves. Can you see how effective this might be? It might separate two people with no further interaction between both. Secrecy, as mentioned earlier, is a means of control for the narcissist.

Now, here's another strategy that narcissists will use: the silent treatment. This is used to gauge the control they have over you. So, by verbally and emotionally "cutting you off," the narcissist offers you a taste of what life might be without their "false self," aka their charming, godlike, awesome self. Which, lest you be hoodwinked, is, as always, a mere façade. A mask. A veneer hiding the monster that lurks beneath. Ready to appear without warning at any given moment.

So, the reason that the narcissist or narcissists in your life ignore, belittle and devalue you is because they hope that it plays on your fear of being alone. In a codependent state, it likely will be effective. Why? Because as yet, you most likely have either extremely little to no self esteem. Your worth is tied up in relation to the narcissist or narcissists. Do you see now how people pleasing at whatever cost can do? And by no means should you feel any shame in this. It takes courage to heal from this kind of abuse. And bottom line is that we have simply been decent, good human beings to a large degree. Who have been taken advantage of.

A little more on the silent treatment from your narcissist or narcissists: It's their hope that by them enacting their silent narcissistic rage against you, that they will force you into submission and into being the good little "narcissistic supply" they need. A little more about "narcissistic supply" shortly. I promise.

Finally, why does the silent treatment potentially work so well on people like you and formerly me? It's because sensitive, empathic people, (who also tend to have no healthy boundaries) are wired to respond to and attempt to soothe the emotions of the people around us, especially those we love. For the record, even after you have healed and are thriving, you are still going to be a decent person. That won't change.

Now, moving onto what I know you've been waiting for: Just what is this "narcissistic supply"?

In essence the narcissist is the mental equivalent of an alcoholic: insatiable. Ironically, they may also actually be alcoholics. My brother is. The narcissistic husband of Margaret Keane, the famous painter, Walter Keane, as portrayed in the film "Big Eyes" also was an alcoholic. Narcissists are sometimes children who have had at least one alcoholic parent. So, the narcissist directs their whole behaviour and life, to obtain pleasurable titbits of attention. Which embeds them in a coherent, completely biased, picture of themselves. Which they use to regulate their changeable sense of self-worth and self-esteem.

To elicit constant interest, they project to others that fabricated, fictitious version of themselves, that "false self", everything the narcissist is not: omniscient, omnipotent, charming, intelligent, rich, or well-connected.

The narcissist then proceeds to harvest reactions to this projected image from family members, friends, co-workers, neighbours, business partners and from colleagues. If these: the adulation, admiration, attention, fear, respect, applause, affirmation aren't forthcoming, the narcissist demands them, or extorts them. Money, compliments, a favourable critique, an appearance in the media, a sexual conquest are all converted into the same currency in the narcissist's mind. This currency is what is termed "narcissistic supply".

To help you further distinguish between the various components of the process of narcissistic supply:

Trigger: The "trigger" of supply is the person or object that provokes the source into yielding narcissistic supply by confronting the source with information about the narcissist's "false self".

Source: The source of narcissistic supply is the person that provides the narcissistic supply.

Narcissistic supply is the reaction of the source to the trigger. Publicity (celebrity or notoriety, being famous or being infamous) is a trigger of narcissistic supply because it provokes people to pay attention to the narcissist (in other words, it moves sources to provide the narcissist with narcissistic supply). Publicity can be obtained by exposing oneself, by creating something, or by provoking attention. The narcissist resorts to all three repeatedly (as drug addicts do to secure their daily dose). A mate or a companion is one such source of narcissistic supply.

But the picture is more complicated. There are two categories of narcissistic supply and their sources:

The primary narcissistic supply is attention, in both its public forms (fame, notoriety, infamy, celebrity) and its private, interpersonal, forms (adoration, adulation, applause, fear, repulsion). It is important to understand that attention of any kind: positive or negative constitutes primary narcissistic supply. Infamy is as sought after as fame, being notorious is as good as being renowned.

To the narcissist his "achievements" can be imaginary, fictitious, or only apparent, as long as others believe in them. Appearances count more than substance, what matters is not the truth but it's perception.

Triggers of primary narcissistic supply include, apart from being famous (celebrity, notoriety, fame, infamy) having an air of mystique (when the narcissist is considered to be mysterious), having sex and deriving from it a sense of masculinity/virility/femininity, and being close or connected to political, financial, military, or spiritual power or authority or yielding them.

Sources of primary narcissistic supply are all those who provide the narcissist with narcissistic supply on a casual, random basis.

Secondary narcissistic supply includes: leading a normal life (a source of great pride for the narcissist), having a secure existence (economic safety, social acceptability, upward mobility), and obtaining companionship.

Thus, having a mate, possessing conspicuous wealth, being creative, running a business (transformed into a pathological narcissistic space), possessing a sense of anarchic freedom, being a member of a group or collective, having a professional or other reputation, being successful, owning property and flaunting one's status symbols: all constitute secondary narcissistic supply as well.

Sources of secondary narcissistic supply are all those who provide the narcissist with narcissistic supply on a regular basis: spouse, friends, colleague, business partners, teachers, neighbours, and so on.

I hope that by now, my dear friend, the veil has fallen from over your eyes. That you can now see things as they actually are: which is that you are simply one of a "harem", as it were, of nothing more than narcissistic supply. The narcissist or narcissists in your life are after entertainment: a snack, or meal. It's up to you to change that. It's up to you to do the work inside of yourself so that it's possible for that to happen. You do have it in you.

It's not going to be easy: it's a journey that must be taken, however long it takes. Your inner child has been wounded, likely the child in you that was not validated, not loved in the truest, unconditional sense of the word. Part of healing is letting your inner child know that it has always been worthy, it has always been enough, and that it has never been it's fault that it was abused in the horrific manner that it was. And oh so importantly, that it can let go of all the guilt and shame.

To assist you in this regard, I highly recommend looking up Lisa A. Romano's videos on YouTube that address this. Because, my dear friend, yes, you are in an adult body now, but that wounded adult child still carries the damage. Your inner child has to heal so that you can move forward and truly thrive. And truly begin the journey to what's termed self love recovery. Yes, there's going to be some crying. But, you know what? That's okay. Because the huge relief, the huge weight that finally lifts from off you for probably the first time in your entire life makes it worth it. For the first time, that wounded child isn't going to be ignored. It's going to be validated. It's going to understand that what's happened to it has nothing to do with it's worthiness. That it never did. Seriously beautiful, awesome stuff, my dear friend.

3

NARCISSISTIC FAMILIES

At this point, I feel it would be of some benefit to go into some detail about the whole dysfunctional "harem" connected to the narcissist. Especially is this the case in a family with a narcissistic parent. A dysfunctional family, where abuse and dysfunction is so much the norm, that no one blinks an eye at it.

The one who picks up on it the most is the person known as the family "scapegoat", also the family truth teller. In my own "family" scenario, this is the category I personally fall into. Generally, we are the ones who walk away. Sooner or later, enough is enough, and we start looking for answers to the pain we've suffered from for so long. On the positive, we are the ones who heal, go "no contact" with the narcissist, along with other toxic and dysfunctional biological family members. And who then proceed to move on with our lives. With our own family. Oh. And go on to have fulfilling, rewarding, successful lives.

We have been the emotional dumping recipient for the narcissistic parent, along with the partner/spouse and generally other children. This is because actually, we are the most emotionally sensitive family member. We are full of empathy and kindness. Of course, this is used against us, in effect.

It could be that the family "scapegoat" is the youngest child, as in my case. It's apparently also quite possible that it may also be the eldest child. When it is the eldest child, it's due to the fact that they have been around the longest. They know the most dirt about the narcissist. They know more secrets than any of the other children. In other words, they're the largest threat to the true, vile self of the narcissist coming to light.

Which, of course, is the greatest fear of the narcissist. Exposure of their real lowlife self. Hence, the use of what's referred to as "smear campaigns". You might have heard the saying that if you throw enough dirt, it will stick. When it comes to the narcissist, this is what they'll do to the goodhearted truth teller, the "scapegoat". If this has happened to you, bear in mind the best reaction is no reaction. The narcissist wants your reaction. In fact, they're counting on it. They're rubbing their hands gleefully in anticipation.

Bear in mind that hopefully any decent, fairminded person would see through this. Anyone who truly knew you as a person shouldn't fall for it. That being said, narcissists are good at what they do. However, if the people the narcissist or narcissists in your life "smear campaign" you to do happen to stop having anything to do with you, taking it on board as if it's factual, they might be of a calibre you'd be better off not having in your life.

Sometimes, those who have listened to the narcissists smear campaign end up seeing the true colours of the narcissist, and also end up realising what was conveyed to them about you was wrong. In some instances, people have ended up even apologising for believing it in the first place. In any case, you will know where they stand in your life. Soon, after you've healed, you're going to be amazed at the people who you seem to attract as friends. You'll find yourself connecting on a deeper level with people. Who are some truly beautiful souls.

After I'd written a book about my childhood years, it got to my narcissistic mother. She tried to guilt and shame me. Via text message. Because in the book, I'd mentioned an incident where my narcissistic personality disordered brother had self abused in front of me. I was all of about six or seven years of age when the incident occurred. It didn't work to the extent she anticipated, I don't think. She texted me that I had to put something dirty in it. I replied that she made me sick. Then she tried another tactic with secrecy, as if it was something I should not have made any mention of.

I was beginning to wake up at this point. I'd put the truth out there, and this didn't even bother me. I was beyond it. As they say: If people want you to write nicely about them, they should have behaved better. Or words to that effect. One thing's for sure, I exposed her true self in that book. And I'm glad that I did. No regrets whatsoever.

On a sad note, the family "scapegoat", the family truth teller tends to be the one who suffers the most. They may end up committing suicide. Tragically, some actually have. I personally was on "suicide watch" for an entire weekend in 2008 before going on antidepressants for almost nine years.

As I often say now, none of them cared. None of them. None were anywhere to be found, nor would I have bothered to attempt to reach out to any of them. That's how it is in a narcissist rule the roost dysfunctional family. I recall mentioning to my narcissistic mother about my depression once. Her response was what did I have to be depressed about. As was often the case for a lot of my life, I said nothing by way of response. There was no point in wasting my breath on the cruel, heartless individual who was the very cause of my depression. Who I incorrectly believed for far too long actually loved me.

In contrast, I felt nothing but the utmost respect and appreciation for the wonderful support of two dear friends, along with my wife and daughter, and even the mental health people who came to visit me on the Sunday of that weekend. It truly was the darkest, lowest point in my life. I simply wanted to get in a car and wrap myself around a tree so that my life was over.

There's a likelihood in a family with at least one narcissistic personality disordered parent that one of the children will also become narcissistic personality disordered. This was how it was for me. Being the youngest child, with fourteen more years or more in age between me and the bulk of my siblings, I experienced my brother's abuse along with my mother's. As I mentioned earlier, he is seven years older than me.

This is why I say that you think one narcissist is enough in a family, try two. Or more. At least in the instance of my NPD brother, he has been absent from my life for a lot of it in my older years. However, not in the earliest part. Where the most damage is done. Later on, I likely will divulge more about the trainwreck of a life he has had, and inflicted upon others.

Getting back to the family member known as the enabler. This usually fits the spouse of the narcissistic parent, if they stay together. Anyone else married to a narcissist would get out of that relationship by separating from them, sooner or later, at the very least. Of course, separation and divorce from a narcissist is a whole other nightmare. Legal help in regards to this is a must. From people who aren't fooled by the narcissist. And document everything that's evidence about the narcissist.

Anyone who a narcissist "recruits" to their side, is basically an enabler. They support, defend, and fight for the narcissist. They put up with their behaviour and bail the narcissist out of the catastrophes in their lives. They will accept no criticism in regards to the narcissist. They think they are helping, but aren't. They reinforce the behaviour of the narcissist. Whilst they usually don't have a malicious motive, they are doing whatever to basically avoid the narcissistic personality disordered person spewing onto them with their narcissistic rage upon receiving narcissistic injury.

Because this person helps the narcissist avoid any consequences, there is nothing happening to prevent the narcissist behaving how they do. They, in effect, reward the narcissist for their behaviour. The enabler doesn't know where they begin and the narcissist ends. In other words, there are no boundaries.

My biological father fell into this category. It was always our NPD mother over any of us children. Not once did he ever stand up for me in any way. Not once. And he was as hypocritical as her. Both hugely hypocritical, along with piety and self righteousness. He even seemed to take delight in punishing me. Basically, both of them were in cahoots. As I write this, they are both now very elderly, and both are now permanently in homes.

I see these enablers as gutless cowards. They have such misplaced loyalty to the narcissist. The wellbeing of the narcissist is more important than their own wellbeing. Which is just what the narcissist craves. I would rather have had a real man for a father, one who stood up for not only himself to her, but also his children. I never had any relationship with my biological parents. (As mentioned in more detail in "Surviving Childhood") Apart from a dysfunctional, emotionally and psychologically abusive, disconnected one, that is.

There is also what is known as the golden child. The golden child is spineless. Make no mistake about it. They also cannot handle evidence. That the way they are thinking is wrong. They understand themselves far less than the "scapegoat" truth teller child. They also will direct their anger at the wrong people. Often this will be the "scapegoat" truth teller child. The blame will be directed at this child because they pointed out what reality is. The golden child can't handle reality. They go back into the dysfunctional family. Why? Because the basic thinking of the golden child is along the lines of this: "Wipe reality out. Make me rich. I don't care."

The golden child doesn't mind offering whatever is deemed necessary to appease the narcissistic parent, regardless of the consequence and hurt to another person in the process. In some instances, the golden child is told by the narcissistic parent that they are loved more than the other children. Also, sadly, they are often the one involved in an incestuous relationship with the narcissistic parent. Which may have a flow on effect in that they will abuse a sibling or others in a similar way.

A personal instance I can relate involves my golden child sister, the only girl in the family. Eighteen years older than me. I know that she took on a lot of responsibility at a young age. I know that as a daughter of a narcissistic mother, this messed up her life relationship wise. She ended up on her own as a single parent with four very young children at the time this happened at. And never found anyone else afterwards. This took place at about the end of 1990.

Upon getting the book I wrote about my childhood years via my niece (another wolf in sheep's clothing) she eagerly passed it onto narcissistic personality disordered mother so that said mother could contact me. (As I mentioned before, in part). Now, the part that shows the spinelessness on her part is that none of this was mentioned to me personally by her. However, via my wife, I found out that golden child sister had commented that she had never read such rubbish.

Do you see the denial in that? Do you also see the spinelessness of it? Not to mention that the golden child "confides" in the "scapegoat" truth teller child when they can't handle the narcissistic parent. This happened with me, too. It was like suddenly: "Oh, she's being "nice"." Only because she had to get it off her chest. Which was what she admitted in her own words via text. That if she didn't vent, she'd go nuts. It was done via text message at the time. Why? Because she had become paid carer of narcissistic personality disordered mother. She'd gone back into the parental home. And carer of enabling father, too, prior to him going into a home. As he went into a home first, due to more and more problems stemming from his advanced dementia.

It's interesting to note, however, that after she had been left on her own with four young children, she went away from her biological family members. Choosing to instead go where her former husband's family members were. Doesn't that in itself speak volumes?

My golden child sister in recent years has even made revealing remarks in regards to the selling of the parental home after their demise. I realised this upon reflection. Although she tried to lighten it up with laughing about how it wouldn't be worth much, it has come through that her basic thinking is precisely that of the malignant golden child: "Wipe reality out. Make me rich. I don't care".

Whereas in my instance, I want nothing from any of them. Why? Because it's simply not worth the price attached. The "strings". And there's always strings attached in this type of dysfunctional family dynamics. Where abuse has always been the norm. And the fact that I've never had a sense of entitlement.

In other words, I prefer to say that none of this is okay. I am simply done with the dysfunction, abuse, and any attached to it. My silence in having gone no contact with them speaks this. My actions say that I have boundaries. I am going to stick to those boundaries. Also, that I am quite okay with leaving my older siblings to deal with it. Because, nothing else is going to wake them up to it. Let them deal with narcissistic personality disordered mother. It's their choice. There's always going to be the twisted honour your parents concept. And what goes along with that. So be it. I gave up myself for forty years for nothing. I have moved on.

This is important to realise, so I am going to clarify it for you, my dear friend: If you are what's known as the "scapegoat" truth teller child of the narcissistic family, in your adult life you will "rebel". You are searching for a new path, because you always felt the reality that you weren't a part of this family. You also feel genuine anger as you wake up that you deserved better.

You most likely were the "quiet" child who picked up on how distracted your narcissistic parent and spouse/partner were. So you didn't ask or expect anything from them. I know that that was precisely how I was. However, you always have been grounded.

On the positive side: You, yes, you, the "scapegoat" truth teller child are so sincere, so genuine. Your integrity remains in tact. And whilst the golden child is completely insincere in anything they do for others, you are anything but that. In fact, you are altruistic.

The sad thing is this: Both the golden child and the "scapegoat" truth teller children were punished. Both have trauma. The difference is that if you are the "scapegoat" truth teller child of the family, you have massive amounts of courage. Whereas the golden child doesn't. Not only that, but the golden child is always relying on what other people can do for them.

The "scapegoat" truth teller child would self annihilate unless they have either something and/or someone to hold onto apart from their narcissistic parent and enabling partner/spouse along with the dysfunctional siblings. I speak from experience that this is most definitely so.

The golden child can also be known as the "split" child. Why? Because the golden child is vilified sometimes, fawned over at other times. Now, it's crucial to understand that the narcissistic parent "fawning" over the golden child is just that. Meaning it is in no way sincere. Ever. Period. The narcissistic parent can't love, and is incapable of love. Therefore, how could it be any other way?

Also, one key difference between the golden child "split" child and the "scapegoat" truth teller child is that the golden child "split" child continues to people please. Yes, they are a people pleaser. That's why if anyone gets out of this dysfunctional narcissistic family mess, it's going to be the "scapegoat" truth teller child. Why? Because, for a start, we have the most courage of any of the children of a narcissist. So, when we wake up to the full horror, to the reality of the entire mess we were involuntarily a part of, we want out of it. We then cease people pleasing.

Connected to this is that even in our childhood we at no time even felt a part of this "family". We always felt isolated. Like we didn't belong in this "family". In fact, I even recall asking at some point in my childhood if I was adopted. To which my narcissistic personality disordered mother told me that I hadn't been. I will mention now that my enabling father was one month off turning fifty one years of age when I was born. And my narcissistic personality disordered mother was almost forty two years of age when she gave birth to me.

That being so, I can remember the "scapegoat" blame as if any of it was my fault growing up. The excuse making, in reality. One example: "We were old when we had you." As if that excused their lack of interest in me, or doing anything remotely emotionally connected with me. I realise now, of course, that neither one of them was capable of being anything other than emotionally detached and disconnected. And basically horrible by nature.

My narcissistic personality disordered mother had a hysterectomy not long after having me. What do you think I internalised blame wise? Yes, that it was my fault. (blame shifting) What remaining teeth she had fell out after having me. What do you think I internalised blame wise? Again, yes. Somehow, it was my fault. All my life, she always only ever had false teeth. There they'd sit each night in the bathroom, in a glass of water overnight.

Which brings me to something you need to know about narcissists: Their self esteem is so shaky. That's why they constantly have to prop it up with their "false self" fabricated ego. They actually can't handle when you point anything out about them that is of any negative nature. This happened with the false teeth. I recall taking her off in front of her, doing "gummy" speak (without teeth). I can recall the horror in her eyes, whilst she simultaneously covered over her mouth. This was when I was married and she was visiting. I guess I was in that "rebel" stage. It was around the same time that I sent her that letter calling out her hypocrisy. The letter I mentioned earlier.

Okay, now lastly, moving onto what are referred to as the flying monkeys. These are people who fight on behalf of the narcissist, who defend the narcissist, and who the narcissist has recruited to be on their side against their targeted victims in "smear campaigns". The term comes from "The Wizard Of Oz" where the wicked witch sent out flying monkeys to do her bidding and attack people on her behalf. Precisely what narcissists do. They poison the person's minds with "victim" stories that portrays the real victim in a negative light, thus incensing the person, who then becomes a "flying monkey". Can they be dysfunctional, toxic, manipulative biological family members? If you hadn't worked out the answer to that already from what I've already disclosed so far, the answer is a resounding yes.

Most non narcissistic people have no prior experience with narcissists. Due to that, they are misled, sucked into believing the narcissist's lies, yes lies about the other person. It can be done as a pre emptive strike on the part of a narcissist. Before the true victim (truth teller) can reveal any truths to others about the narcissist. Remember how manipulative and victim sounding a narcissist can be. It can take people some time to wake up to the truth about you. To realise that they were lied to.

The best way to deal with these people is to not have anything to do with them. No contact. Sooner or later, in some instances, such people have contacted the true victim and said that they were sorry. Is it hard at the same time as you might be healing from narcissistic abuse that you are experiencing a "smear campaign" from a narcissist along

with any "flying monkeys" who believe this assassination
of your character? Yes. However, one thing that's
worth you bearing in mind, my dear friend is this: It took
both you and I some time to wake up to the true nature of
the narcissist or narcissists in our lives, didn't it?

4

THE NARCISSIST MENTALITY

"Is this person really a narcissist"? you might be asking. Along with, is it true that they really cannot and will not change? The answer to the second question is simple: Yes, it is true. How can someone who will not acknowledge that there's even a problem with them change? How can someone who has no self reflection, because if they do, it triggers narcissistic injury because their false self collapses change? Please, though: Don't simply take my word for it. Feel free to look up online how any narcissist who actually went to therapy for any help is in and out for decades with little or no change.

I've been there. Believe me, I wanted likely as desperately as you, if not more so, for it to be possible for my mother and brother to change. I clung to the delusion that my mother loved me. I also clung to the hope that she might change. That she might apologise for all the harm she'd ever done. Guess what? Nothing changed. There's never been any accountability from either one. Avoiding and evading accountability is their specialty. I will tell you this, though, my dear friend: Once I let go of those damaging beliefs, it was liberating. Things improved from that point on.

To help you with the narcissist check list some more, here are some things that a narcissist will never do, and some things a narcissist always will do. Are you ready? Okay, here we go.

They will never take responsibility. Why? Any type of

responsibility in one's life opens them up to criticism and judgement, and a narcissist can't handle shame or blame. They will schedule their entire lives to avoid any situation where they must step up to the plate.

They avoid any true emotion. Why? Whilst a narcissist may say nearly anything to keep the attention on themselves, they will go out of their way to avoid any sense of true emotion. They hide their feelings to avoid vulnerability, but aren't above playing the victim to get their way.

They are guilty of name dropping. Why? Anything that can make a narcissist look better or more important is a win in their book. And name dropping gives them exactly the illusion of that. (Which Hyacinth Bucket does in "Keeping Up Appearances" constantly)

They never apologise. Why? It's hard to admit when we are wrong, and harder when someone has themselves convinced that they are always right (the narcissist). Their sense of superiority leads them to believe they are better than those around them, and they would never stoop to admitting fault and apologising for their actions.

They will never act selflessly in any way. Why? Narcissists lack empathy. That, combined with their inflated sense of entitlement means that they would never even consider a selfless act. If they are not going to benefit from it in some way, they are not going to spend their valuable time and energy carrying it out.

They can manipulate any conversation into being about them. Why? A narcissist needs to feel like the attention is on them, so when the conversation veers away from this all too important topic, they are extremely skilled at bringing it right back to a story centred around them once again.

They avoid self reflection. Why? Narcissism is often a trait found in individuals who were irrepairably damaged at some stage in their life. The act of self refection would require them to show a level of vulnerability that they are not willing to invite into their lives. They rarely seek any type of counselling and avoid honest communication and accountability.

Their social media accounts include a ton of friends, and not a single bad picture. Why? Social media for a narcissist is all about status. They want to look as good as they can for as many people as possible. It's a way to brag of their perfect life, and appear extremely popular in the process.

Okay, so there you have it. I hope that if you were left in any doubt, that you now have any doubts removed. Why is this so important? Because being in any kind of constant relationship with a narcissist takes it's toll on your energy and mental health. And you may well be so damaged from them that you literally can't think straight. The narcissist capitalises on your being in a state of confusion. Which is why you need to find out as much as possible about their unchangeable, harm inflicting condition. Now, my dear friend, onto something that can frustrate you like crazy: How the narcissist evades being questioned. Because, now you know that there's never going to be any accountability from them, you know they evade any questioning from you. You're bound to have experienced it. And as it can be so downright confusing, let's try and remove some of that from your already far too battered mind.

I'm going to endeavour to explain it from the narcissists point of view, as I do feel that this is the most effective way for you to understand precisely what you have been dealing with for however long. How warped their state of thinking actually is. Also, what you will continue to deal with until you leave them behind for good, and move on with your life.

Before I do so, though, my dear friend, please know that there is absolutely no judgement on this end from me whatsoever. Nothing other than massive support for you. I've been through what you have. Perhaps in a different relationship, but I had decades of this kind of thing that wreaked it's havoc on me.

Bottom line: The sooner you educate yourself to the monster or monsters you've been dealing with, and understand fully the ramifications of continuing to do so: How serious a threat these people are to your welfare and wellbeing, even to your very life, how cutting them out of your life by means of no contact whatsoever (along with any enablers and flying monkeys connected to them) is not only necessary as your end goal but will signal you've healed significantly, not to mention the best, thriving part of your life has begun – well, the better it will be for you, my dear friend.

This is the narrative that more or less is running in the mind of the narcissist when you question them:

Don't question me. You're not allowed. It's an affront to me believing I'm superior to you or whoever else has the audacity to do the same. It's also an insult to my feelings that I am not accountable. Ever. If you didn't know, (and let's face it: how would you, when you're so inferior to me?) for me this is without exception: Feelings are facts. My feelings. Duh. Not yours. They never matter. They never will.

So even if you think you've asked me politely, I perceive you're questioning me in a critical manner. How dare you ask me where I've been. Are you suggesting to me that I'm not allowed to do whatever I want, whenever I want? That I am somehow accountable to you? (Despite the fact being that I am superior to you.)

When you start with deliberate questioning, I dislike your challenging me, but so long as you're also providing me with fuel at the same time, my fury isn't ignited. You are irritated, you are annoyed as you ask me why I didn't do this or why I didn't do that. Fuel is fuel. The core emotion that fuels me at any given time is envy, (a primitive form of hatred). Contempt is one way I express this. Hatred another. I want to destroy everything beautiful. I am either all good or all bad in my polarised way of thinking.

So, what do I do? I recognise your challenging behaviour and identify that this must be addressed and my superiority exerted but at the same time I also see that there is an opportunity for me to gain more fuel from you.

At this point, you likely think that since my fury has not been ignited (yet) that I could accept the fuel provided and admit that I was in the wrong, explain what has happened and allow the matter to be resolved. A normal person may do this and you, as an empathic individual, would say your piece and with the agreement and resolution being achieved, you will draw a line under it and move on. Such a scenario is no good to me. Why? You have challenged me and whilst the fury has not been ignited I must still maintain my superiority and this means rejecting your challenge. This rejection also presents me with an opportunity to draw fuel from you, by denying your assertion and so forth. Thus I assert my superiority and gain fuel.

If you engage in perceived questioning this invariably

ignites my fury. Why? Because you will do it in a fuel-free manner, so that the perceived criticism arising from your questioning wounds me, thus my fury ignites and I lash out in order to demand fuel to heal the wound caused by your criticism. You may have asked me a question, but you did so without any agenda attached to it. However, I do not see it that way. Your simple query of "Oh, where have you been?" is interpreted by me as suggesting that I am not entitled to do what I want without your approval first. It is delivered without fuel and is critical, thus the wounding occurs and the ignition of fury occurs. I must strike back, once again in order to assert my superiority but also to gain fuel from you.

Accordingly, whether you raise questions in an emotional manner, whether you ask them in a straight-forward way, whether you are demanding that I explain myself or that your question is innocuous, you are always going to find that I'll respond in a manner which provokes an argument.

I do not want you questioning me, whether it is deliberate or perceived. You are not permitted by my rules to do so. Once you do, I must reject your challenge, assert my superiority and gain fuel (either because I see the opportunity to do so or because I have to heal the wound). What is the result of this? The deployment of evasion tactics.

This is why you are never able to have a reasonable discussion about something that is concerning you, or why I fly off the handle after a seemingly innocent question you have asked me. Which you find both alarming and bewildering. This is why you find your concerns are not resolved, that you are pushed to a state of heightened emotion, confused, annoyed and frustrated as I point blank refuse to answer what you have asked me. These responses on my part are largely instinctive, a reaction to your challenging behaviour and the prospect/necessity of fuel. I will delight in adding to these instinctive responses by layering them with further manipulation and game-playing.

So, what are these evasion tactics? There are many but below are eight which you will no doubt be familiar with. Now you know that these responses, hitherto unexplained and perplexing, are instinctive responses designed to counter your challenge to my superiority and to cater for my need for fuel. No longer will you scratch your head at why I do these things when you question me and instead you ought now to realise how you are only falling into a trap every time you try to engage me.

Why do you fall into this trap? It is because of your innate empathic traits which cause you to be drawn into my machinations through the evasion tactics. You fall for this because you continue to engage with me for the following reasons:-

You need to secure the reality of what has happened. (the truth seeker)

You want me to see your point of view. (the need to fix)

You want to be heard. (the need to be honest to yourself)

You want resolution. (the need to be decent)

These traits of yours cause you to become entangled every time I deploy the evasion tactics, of which eight are now detailed as follows:

1. Drown You Out

I will talk over you, I will shout over you, I will hurl
insults at you in a blitzkrieg response which is designed to
result in the fact that since you can no longer be heard
then you can no longer challenge me. Hearing is
challenging. I do not want to hear you any longer and
instead I shall draw fuel from your gestures and
expressions as your blanketing response draws your
frustration and anger.

2. Other People

I shift the topic of conversation onto other people in
order to deflect from your attack against me. I will explain
how a colleague works similarly late and never receives any
flak from their spouse in order to make you appear
unreasonable. I will triangulate you by explaining how a
previous partner never made such a fuss about my
spending habits. By comparing you to other people I
engage in my classic act of triangulation, aiming to belittle
you and cause you to talk about those other people rather
than continuing your attack against me.

3. Delivery But Not Content

I will repeatedly interrupt you as I demand to be allowed
to finish. I accuse you of not allowing me to speak my
mind. I tell you that you are judging me before I have been
able to state my case. I remind you not to interrupt me,
not to raise your voice at me, and demand that you lower
your voice or change your tone. None of this of course
addresses the content of what you are wanting to discuss
with me, but instead I deflect by getting you to defend

yourself by saying you are not interrupting, you are not raising your voice and so forth. Your challenge becomes lost as you are caught up in these sideshows, and all the while the emotion pours from you.

4. Early Resolution

This is a classic tactic of both the lesser and the mid-ranger. The lesser, lacking the articulate nature to continue the verbal sparring decides to call time on the "discussion," and thus end the attack. I will announce that the discussion is at an end, and will sign off with one last act, which will draw a sudden surge of fuel from you. I may push you and bellow that the matter is over, or possibly lash out with fists and spit in your face that I have had enough of talking. Your shocked and hurt response provides that jet of fuel that I require and so I then withdraw, satisfied that I have asserted myself and have instinctively avoided any further wounding.

If I am the mid-ranger, I will declare: "There is nothing more to discuss." "I have made my point and that is the end of it." "This ends now."

I will then withdraw and dole out a silent treatment, gaining fuel after the event and having protected myself, perhaps when I felt that the situation was slipping away from me, by withdrawing from the continuing challenge or criticism.

5. The Shift

I will turn the discussion onto something else completely. I may talk about some issue arising at work, point out that the exterior of the house needs a bit of paint or that I am thinking about buying a new car. You will try and shift the topic back to what you want to discuss, but I will keep tugging it off topic again as I demonstrate my control over you. All the while your emotional responses provide me with fuel.

6. The Outgunning

You think I have done something wrong? Luckily for me, I know of plenty of other things which you have done (in my mind) that are far worse and therefore I will commence my own inquisition of you about your behaviour in order to demonstrate that you are the one who is in the wrong and should be subjected to questioning, not me. You feel the need to get to the truth of the matter and therefore you are derailed from advancing your questioning of me, as you are forced into defending yourself.

7. How Could You?

How could you treat me in this manner after all that I have done for you? After the week I have had at work? Knowing that my pet has just died? Knowing that my basketball team lost the final? I will roll out one of the typical pity plays by pointing out that I have either done so much for you and this is the thanks that I get and/or you are a heartless cow who is kicking me when I am down. Either way, it prompts you to justify your approach and deflects from what you have been trying to discuss.

8. Pest

Why won't you leave me alone? I just want a simple and quiet life (oh, the hypocrisy) but you just won't let me, will you? You have to keep pestering me with questions all of the time, just shut up and leave me be. This is often used when you engage in perceived questioning, as my abrupt response to you just asking, "How are you?" Which of course then leaves you upset and bewildered.

Okay, so there you have it. That's some insight for you, my dear friend. From inside the mind of the narcissist in your life. Do you see now why there's no other option then to run from such a deranged individual? However, you have to be oh so careful as to the narcissist knowing anything about what you plan to do. Never for one moment underestimate what they will do. Never forget that they wish to utterly ruin you, that they would delight in ruining you. They literally feel they have nothing to lose.

Please don't let this disturb you or deter you. All it means, my dear friend, is this: You need to learn as much as you can about narcissism, and you need to do this in privacy. Regarding healing from the narcissist who has abused you: It's best to heal away from them. If at all possible. Obviously, if you are living with a narcissist, they are going to be doing whatever they can to ensure you are stuck with them. It's in their interest to keep you chained to them. You do need to break the shackles. However, you need to be cool, calm, and collected in organising this. And when you do get away from them, you need to be sure there is no way they can find or contact you. You must leave no trail whatsoever that leads to you.

Will this be hard? Yes. Is it worth it? Yes. The other

alternative makes one shudder. If the graveness of the situation hasn't fully hit you yet, or you are in some doubt that it really is as bad as I've suggested it is, please, my dear friend, do your due diligence and research. Look up online what people who've been in your shoes have to say. I know in the instance of my own narcissistic personality disordered brother, just what he did to his own wife, and in front of their very young son. It's beyond horrific. Beyond horrific.

At this point, I am going to tell you to look up on YouTube the following four people's channels, and watch their videos, listen to what they explain, and get yourself healed, my dear friend. These four people I credit to having helped me the most of anyone. They walk the walk, they talk the talk. They've all been there. If you have depression, if you have Complex PTSD, if you have low self esteem and low self worth, you're in for a treat. I had all of those things for the first approximately forty years of my life. All of those things are a result of narcissistic abuse. These people changed that, and can do the same for you, my dear friend. So, here they are:

Lisa A. Romano (Lisa had a narcissistic parent and enabling codependent parent along with an ex narcissistic husband)

Margaret Paul (Margaret had a narcissistic borderline mother)

Ross Rosenberg (Ross was married to two narcissistic women before his third marriage)

Jerry Wise (Jerry's take on family

enmeshment/narcissism and his insights are unique, beneficial and resonate profoundly)

Those four people resonated the most with me, and helped me more than any others. I credit especially Lisa and Margaret with helping get rid of my depression. (I got off antidepressants after almost nine years on them) And have been in the best place of my life since. Also, I credit all four of them for helping to take my power back by helping me establish healthy boundaries, so that I would no longer allow myself to me gaslighted, manipulated, or drawn into the toxic dynamics that are my biological family.

Yes, you are going to cry. And that's okay, my dear friend. You are going to cry as you let go of the baggage that kept you tied to the narcissist or narcissists in your life. Then, it gets better. It truly does. I also suggest one more person to look up their channel on YouTube. (Especially for those of you who are currently either in or who have ever been in a romantic relationship with a narcissist). And she's an Australian like me. Her name is Melanie Tonia Evans. I mention her, because I found her considerably later than the other four, who had already helped me immensely. She rocks. So, what are you waiting for? It's time for you to fully educate yourself. It's time for you to heal. Go do it, my dear friend. You've got this.

5

STEPS TO HEAL & WHY YOU'VE FELT TRAPPED

Now, my dear friend: It's time to outline some steps that are necessary to go through for your own personal healing process from the soul destroying narcissistic abuse you've fallen victim to. Yes, you are the real victim. I know I mentioned it's important to learn all you can about narcissism. That is the very first thing to do. To educate yourself.

In a humorous way, here's my super quick narcissist education for you: (not too long ago there's no way that I'd be able to see the humour in any of this – but that's how far you can progress) Despite the fact that the narcissist presents themselves as the best thing since sliced bread, they are actually a pile of dung. (It's funny because it's true – And by no means does this invalidate anything you've been through, my dear friend. Nothing but healing hugs being sent your way. Goodness knows, you've been trapped in a psychological warzone). As was I.

A more serious way of putting it is as follows: To a narcissist: What do you want to be when you grow up? Narcissist: A destroyer. I want to destroy anything good and beautiful. The thing is this: The narcissist didn't wait to grow up to do it. They started early.

I realise, my dear friend, that I'm labouring on this, but only because it's imperative that you realise the hopelessness of the situation related to being in any kind of engaged relationship with a soul destroying narcissist. Now, let's get you healed. I am about to go over some steps related to your healing. Whilst these are particularly pertinent for if you have been raised by a narcissist, they also apply to any relationship with a narcissist. So, please, my dear friend, take your time going through this, and let it hit you. And allow it to hit you hard.

Accept That Your Narcissist/s Won't Change

One of the most difficult challenges you face is accepting that your narcissist in all likelihood will never change. If the narcissist in your life finds a way to make personal progress toward a healthier state of being, great, but you should assume they won't. Narcissists rarely change, and if they are acting nicer it is most likely a manipulative manoeuvre. Holding out hope that your narcissist will finally give you the unconditional love you have craved your whole life is natural, but it is a false dream that makes you vulnerable to further abuse and keeps you from moving on.

For me personally when I let go of the delusion that my mother would change at some point, and apologise for all the wrong she had done to me, it was so freeing. So liberating. A heavy load, a heavy weight and burden I'd carried all my life was gone. Pronto.

So my mother would never love me unconditionally: but knowing that it wasn't my fault, that it was never my fault, it had never been my fault, knowing that it was a deluded fantasy that I had held onto for so long that damaged me: Massive peace and relief swept over me. Once that emotional connection was gone for good, she lost her power over me. She had no power over me. After having had it for over four decades. Like that, it was gone. That's powerfully awesome, isn't it, my dear friend? I want that for you too. You can have that right now as you process this. The way that the narcissist or narcissists in your life act and behave has no reflection on your lovability. It never did. All it boils down to is that they simply are incapable of any form of real love.

Recognize Your Narcissist's Enabler

If you have a narcissist parent, chances are you also have an enabling one. (This may also apply to someone else you know connected to the narcissist in your life. Even if the narcissist isn't your parent). What does that really mean? (I know I've made some mention re enablers already, but it's always good to elaborate, and reiterate. Especially when you've been crazymade, confused and drained by a narcissist, who has you questioning yourself.) By going along with and/or excusing the narcissist's abusive behavior, enablers essentially "normalize" and sustain it. Sometimes enablers also act as "flying monkeys" by assisting the narcissist in their dirty work, condoning and perpetuating their abuse. By not naming the abuse and not protecting their children from it, enablers become complicit, even if they are also victimized by it.

Sometimes forgiving the enabling parent can be as hard or harder than forgiving the narcissist parent. People with NPD have a personality disorder formed in early childhood apparently caused by a devastating deprivation. Although the narcissist may behave monstrously, you may find yourself feeling worse about the more functional enabling parent. You may wonder why that parent excused the narcissist and didn't protect you from abuse, and you may feel terribly betrayed by his/her complicity. I know I did. Actually, I still do.

In my eyes, my enabling father will never be anything other than a coward. As well as a pious, self righteous hypocrite. Who, although not NPD, was never there for me in any real way. So, you see, my dear friend, I've mourned not only the loss of my NPD mother, but also my enabling father. The parents I never had. The parents who were incapable of loving me unconditionally. Nonetheless, that's empowering for moving on with your life.

Recognize the Roles in Your Family

Were you a scapegoat (truth teller) or the golden child? Have you acted at times as a flying monkey? Roles are often fluid in the narcissistic family, depending on the narcissist's agenda. Perhaps you have been the golden child and also scapegoated. Because the narcissist maintains control by creating divisions (divide and conquer) among family members, you may feel alienated from your other parent and siblings. Perhaps you feel betrayed by them. It is important to remember that all of you have been part of a warped system orchestrated by the dominant narcissist in the family singularly to serve his or her needs at the expense of others. On some level you have all been fighting to survive with the roles you have been cast in.

The most powerful defense against the narcissist is a unified front against them. If you can find mutual understanding and unity with your other family members, that can be an empowering way to shut down the narcissist's abuse, as well as a profound source of validation for what you have been through. However, if your other parent or siblings are not trustworthy or open to talking about the narcissism in your family, you need above all to protect yourself and limit contact with them.

Sadly, this is the case the majority of the time.

Assert Boundaries

Narcissists constantly violate boundaries. They see others, particularly their children, as extensions of themselves to control and manipulate. As the golden child your job is to reflect what the narcissist wishes to see in themself and wishes to project to the world. As the scapegoat, your job is to take the blame for the family's problems, endure the narcissist's worst abuse, and handle unreasonable responsibilities. Either way, as the narcissist's child you are objectified, not respected as a person with your own identity. The narcissist tells you what you think and feel and insists on your compliance with their version of "reality" no matter how absurd, false, or harmful.

One of the most difficult and important things you must do for yourself as a survivor is to establish healthy boundaries. Understanding what that means and getting comfortable doing it can take considerable time and practice for the child of a narcissist. The first place to start is with the narcissistic parent and possibly other family members.

Attune with Your Feelings

As the child of a narcissistic parent, you have been systematically trained to ignore your feelings, even to fear and hate them. Your feelings are a direct threat to the narcissist parent because they are likely to conflict with what they need, believe, and demand. In the narcissistic family, only the narcissist's feelings matter, and everyone else's must be sublimated or outright crushed through ridicule, shame, rage, and other forms of attack.

Perhaps the most important thing to do for yourself

toward healing is to reconnect with your feelings. They are there, and they always have been. Let them in, listen to them, carry them with respect. In your feelings you will locate yourself and your way through and out of the narcissist's "alternative facts" world. Since you have been violated in innumerable ways by your parent(s), you will have to navigate through intense hurt and anger. Most narcissists constantly project their own bankrupt motives and emotions onto others and blame others for or even accuse them of their own abusive behavior, so at first you may not know what you really feel versus what you have been brainwashed to believe. As you learn to attune to your feelings, be patient. Try not to judge yourself. Feelings are feelings are feelings. They deserve, and in the scheme of things insist upon, recognition and respect.

Don't Blame Yourself

Especially if you've been scapegoated in your family, you are likely to automatically blame yourself and feel guilt for things beyond your control or responsibility. Narcissists are experts at deflecting and projecting blame onto others. If they raged at you and you stood up for yourself, you attacked them. If they punched you, you drove them to it. One of the best ways to break your unhealthy family dynamics is to stop blaming yourself for what was never your responsibility or fault to begin with. If your relationship with a narcissist isn't a family one, the same applies. It's always someone else's fault with a narcissist. Whereas a more balanced person, even if still codependent, accepts accountability for their actions.

Stop Hurting Yourself

Along with not blaming yourself, chances are you need to stop patterns of self-abuse. As someone raised in a narcissistic family, you are prone to risky, self punishing, and self soothing but destructive behaviors, such as substance abuse and addictions, self-harm, and thrill-seeking. Your self-destructive behavior is an internalization of the narcissistic abuse you grew up with, which is the opposite of the narcissist's externalization of their pain. By engaging in such behavior you continue to give the narcissist power over you. You also exacerbate the emotional and physiological trauma you have already endured. Patterns of addiction and self-harm can be extremely hard to break, so seek help and support from people who understand the dynamics of narcissism. These distractions and addictions are what Margaret Paul terms our "self abandonment". They can be a way of self avoidance. In effect, we selfishly hand ourselves over to others and say, "Here I am. You fix me."

Be Aware of Your Attractions with Narcissists

To add further injury to injury, many adult children of narcissists are vulnerable to being drawn into relationships with narcissists beyond their family of origin, including partners, friends, and bosses. It sucks, but there is no shame in this: Repeating the past until we learn from it is the mind-body's way of healing. So pay attention. Learn. Keep educating yourself about narcissism. Develop a fine-tuned narcissist radar, or "nardar." If you get tripped up in unhealthy relationships, forgive yourself and move on. At most, only about one in six people have NPD. Some figures estimate less, but let's face it: Narcissists aren't going to put their hand up and say: Hey, I'm a narcissist, are they? So, yes, it is somewhat of a guess. Still, the point is that there are a lot of non narcissists out there, so please do go and find them.

Honor Your Feelings About Your Narcissist Parent

Most of us love our parents, no matter what, and we

cling to our need for love and validation from them. Your narcissistic parent cannot love you unconditionally the way we all deserve to be loved within our families, and for that matter is capable of no more than fake fleeting empathy. Yet you may still love that parent. Mixed with grief and anger, you may also sympathize with your parent's NPD. It is also possible that you are numb to your parent or too used up to feel love anymore.

Whatever you feel, try not to judge yourself for it. Honor your feelings and let them be your guide in how you choose to interact with your family. Go no contact if that feels like the safest choice. Or operate with firm boundaries and lowered expectations. Narcissist parents, unless they are true sadists, are usually capable of some kind of affection for their children, albeit for their own selfish reasons, at least sometimes. Some may be able to give in ways that you find nurturing or helpful. But don't expect it. With a healthy dose of skepticism, you might wish to take the seemingly good when it comes, as limited as it may be.

Treat Yourself for Narcissistic "Fleas"

Children raised by a narcissist are likely to pick up at least some narcissistic traits or tics, also known as "narcissist fleas." Some become full-blown narcissists themselves, but many merely perpetuate a few behaviors that can be overcome with mindfulness and practice. Take a look at yourself. What triggers you? What do you do that reminds you of your narcissist mother or father? Are you quick to anger? Do you seek attention or control through guilt or manipulation? Could you be more sensitive to other's feelings and perspectives?

The best revenge is a life well-lived. Work on mindfulness and peace in your own life. You can't help how you were raised, but you can work to control how you act now and how you raise your own children.

At this point, I think it's only fair to discuss what exactly is it that has kept you feeling bonded emotionally (despite it being clearly to your detriment) with the narcissist or narcissists in your life. Because, let's face it: If it was possible to simply feel like we could just walk away, we would, right? But, you haven't felt that way. I didn't feel that way. And anyone else who has been stuck in this toxic, dysfunctional abuse cycle hasn't either. Even when physical and sexual abuse are part of the equation. Along with the ongoing emotional, psychological abuse. And, we would love for nothing more than that we could "fix" this disordered person/relationship with them. That's why we've hung around, isn't it?

People are often amazed at their own psychological conditions and reactions. Those with depression are stunned when they remember they've thought of killing themselves. Patients recovering from severe psychiatric disturbances are often shocked as they remember their symptoms and behavior during the episode. A patient with Bipolar Disorder once revealed, "I can't believe I thought I could change the weather through mental telepathy." A common reaction is "I can't believe I did that." What I'm getting at, my dear friend, is this applies very much so to a relationship with a narcissist.

In clinical practice, some of the most surprised and shocked individuals are those who have been involved in controlling and abusive relationships. When the relationship ends, they offer comments such as "I know what he's done to me, but I still love him", "I don't know why, but I want him back", or "I know it sounds crazy, but I miss her". Others have said: "This doesn't make sense. He's got a new girlfriend and he's abusing her too…but

I'm jealous." Friends and relatives are even more amazed and shocked when they hear these comments or witness their loved one returning to an abusive relationship. While the situation doesn't make sense from a social standpoint, does it make sense from a psychological viewpoint? The answer is — Yes.

On August 23rd, 1973 two machine-gun carrying criminals entered a bank in Stockholm, Sweden. Blasting their guns, one prison escapee named Jan-Erik Olsson announced to the terrified bank employees: "The party has just begun." The two bank robbers held four hostages, three women and one man, for the next one hundred and thirty one hours. The hostages were strapped with dynamite and held in a bank vault until finally rescued on August 28th.

After their rescue, the hostages exhibited a shocking attitude considering they were threatened, abused, and feared for their lives for over five days. In their media interviews, it was clear that they supported their captors and actually feared law enforcement personnel who came to their rescue. The hostages had begun to feel the captors were actually protecting them from the police. One woman later became engaged to one of the criminals and another developed a legal defense fund to aid in their criminal defense fees. Clearly, the hostages had "bonded" emotionally with their captors.

While the psychological condition in hostage situations became known as "Stockholm Syndrome" due to the publicity, the emotional "bonding" with captors was a familiar story in psychology. It had been recognized many years before and was found in studies of other hostage, prisoner, or abusive situations such as:

Abused children

Battered/abused women

Prisoners of war

Cult members

Incest victims

Criminal hostage situations

Concentration camp prisoners

Controlling/intimidating relationships

In the final analysis, emotionally bonding with an abuser is actually a strategy for survival for victims of abuse and intimidation. The "Stockholm Syndrome" reaction in hostage and/or abuse situations is so well recognized at this time that police hostage negotiators no longer view it as unusual. In fact, it is often encouraged in crime situations as it improves the chances for survival of the hostages. On the down side, it also assures that the hostages experiencing "Stockholm Syndrome" will not be very cooperative during rescue or criminal prosecution. Local law enforcement personnel have long recognized this syndrome with battered women who fail to press charges, bail their battering husband/boyfriend out of jail, and even physically attack police officers when they arrive to rescue them from a violent assault.

Stockholm Syndrome (SS) can also be found in family, romantic, and interpersonal relationships. The abuser may be a husband or wife, boyfriend or girlfriend, father or mother, or any other role in which the abuser is in a position of control or authority. (The narcissist or narcissists in your life).

It's important to understand the components of Stockholm Syndrome as they relate to abusive and controlling relationships. Once the syndrome is understood, it's easier to understand why victims support, love, and even defend their abusers and controllers. Every syndrome has symptoms or behaviors, and Stockholm Syndrome is no exception. While a clear-cut list has not been established due to varying opinions by researchers and experts, several of these features will be present:

Positive feelings by the victim toward the abuser/controller

Negative feelings by the victim toward family, friends, or authorities trying to rescue/support them or win their release

Support of the abuser's reasons and behaviors

Positive feelings by the abuser toward the victim

Supportive behaviors by the victim, at times helping the abuser

Inability to engage in behaviors that may assist in their release or detachment

Stockholm Syndrome doesn't occur in every hostage or abusive situation. In another bank robbery involving hostages, after terrorizing patrons and employees for many hours, a police sharpshooter shot and wounded the terrorizing bank robber. After he hit the floor, two women picked him up and physically held him up to the window for another shot. As you can see, the length of time one is exposed to abuse/control and other factors are certainly involved.

It has been found that four situations or conditions are present that serve as a foundation for the development of Stockholm Syndrome. These four situations can be found in hostage, severe abuse, and abusive relationships:

The presence of a perceived threat to one's physical or psychological survival and the belief that the abuser would carry out the threat

The presence of a perceived small kindness from the abuser to the victim

Isolation from perspectives other than those of the abuser

The perceived inability to escape the situation

By considering each situation we can understand how Stockholm Syndrome develops in romantic relationships as well as criminal/hostage situations. Looking at each situation:

Perceived threat to one's physical/psychological survival

The perception of threat can be formed by direct, indirect, or witnessed methods. Criminal or antisocial partners can directly threaten your life or the life of friends and family. Their history of violence leads us to believe that the captor/controller will carry out the threat in a direct manner if we fail to comply with their demands. The abuser assures us that only our cooperation keeps our loved ones safe.

Indirectly, the abuser/controller offers subtle threats that you will never leave them or have another partner, reminding you that people in the past have paid dearly for not following their wishes. Hints are often offered such as "I know people who can make others disappear". Indirect threats also come from the stories told by the abuser or controller — how they obtained revenge on those who have crossed them in the past. These stories of revenge are told to remind the victim that revenge is possible if they leave.

Witnessing violence or aggression is also a perceived threat. Witnessing a violent temper directed at a television set, others on the highway, or a third party clearly sends us the message that we could be the next target for violence. Witnessing the thoughts and attitudes of the abuser/controller is threatening and intimidating, knowing that we will be the target of those thoughts in the future.

The "small kindness" perception

In threatening and survival situations, we look for evidence of hope — a small sign that the situation may improve. When an abuser/controller shows the victim some small kindness, even though it is to the abuser's benefit as well, the victim interprets that small kindness as a positive trait of the captor. In criminal/war hostage situations, letting the victim live is often enough. Small behaviors, such as allowing a bathroom visit or providing food/water, are enough to strengthen the Stockholm Syndrome in criminal hostage events.

In relationships with abusers, a card for a specific occasion, a gift (usually provided after a period of abuse), or a special treat are interpreted as not only positive, but evidence that the abuser is not "all bad" and may at some time correct his/her behavior. Abusers and controllers are often given positive credit for not abusing their partner, when the partner would have normally been subjected to verbal or physical abuse in a certain situation. An aggressive and jealous partner may normally become intimidating or abusive in certain social situations, as when an opposite-sex coworker waves in a crowd. After seeing the wave, the victim expects to be verbally battered and when it doesn't happen, that "small kindness" is interpreted as a positive sign.

Similar to the small kindness perception is the perception of a "soft side". During the relationship, the abuser/controller may share information about their past — how they were mistreated, abused, neglected, or wronged. The victim begins to feel the abuser/controller may be capable of fixing their behavior or worse yet, that they (abuser) may also be a "victim". Sympathy may develop toward the abuser and we often hear the victim of Stockholm Syndrome defending their abuser with "I know he fractured my jaw and ribs…but he's troubled. He had a rough childhood." Losers and abusers may admit they need psychiatric help or acknowledge they are mentally disturbed; however, it's almost always after they have already abused or intimidated the victim. The admission is a way of denying responsibility for the abuse.

In truth, personality disorders and criminals have learned over the years that personal responsibility for their violent/abusive behaviors can be minimized and even denied by blaming their bad upbringing, abuse as a child, and now even video games. One murderer blamed his crime on eating too much junk food — now known as the "Twinkie defense". While it may be true that the abuser/controller had a difficult upbringing, showing sympathy for his/her history produces no change in their behavior and in fact, prolongs the length of time you will be abused. While "sad stories" are always included in their apologies — after the abusive/controlling event — their behavior never changes.

Keep in mind: once you become hardened to the "sad stories", they will simply try another approach. I know of no victim of abuse or crime who has heard their abuser say "I'm beating (robbing, mugging, etc.) you because my mother hated me."

Isolation from perspectives other than those of the captor

In abusive and controlling relationships, the victim has the sense they are always "walking on eggshells" — fearful of saying or doing anything that might prompt a violent/intimidating outburst. For their survival, they begin to see the world through the abuser's perspective. They begin to fix things that might prompt an outburst, act in ways they know makes the abuser happy, or avoid aspects of their own life that may prompt a problem. If we only have a dollar in our pocket, then most of our decisions become financial decisions. If our partner is an abuser or controller, then the majority of our decisions are based on our perception of the abuser's potential reaction. We become preoccupied with the needs, desires, and habits of the abuser/controller. This is what's termed codependent, as I previously have made mention of.

Taking the abuser's perspective as a survival technique can become so intense that the victim actually develops anger toward those trying to help them. The abuser is already angry and resentful toward anyone who would provide the victim support, typically using multiple methods and manipulations to isolate the victim from others. Any contact the victim has with supportive people in the community is met with accusations, threats, and/or violent outbursts. Victims then turn on their family — fearing family contact will cause additional violence and abuse in the home. At this point, victims curse their parents and friends, tell them not to call and to stop interfering, and break off communication with others. Agreeing with the abuser/controller, supportive others are now viewed as "causing trouble" and must be avoided. Many victims threaten their family and friends with restraining orders if they continue to "interfere" or try to help the victim in their situation. On the surface it would appear that they have sided with the abuser/controller. In truth, they are trying to minimize contact with situations that might make them a target of additional verbal abuse or intimidation. If a casual phone call from mother prompts a two-hour temper outburst with threats and accusations — the victim quickly realizes it's safer if mother stops calling. If simply telling mother to stop calling doesn't work, for his or her own safety the victim may accuse mother of attempting to ruin the relationship and demand that she stop calling.

In severe cases of Stockholm Syndrome in relationships, the victim may have difficulty leaving the abuser and may actually feel the abusive situation is their fault. In law enforcement situations, the victim may actually feel the arrest of their partner for physical abuse or battering is their fault. Some women will allow their children to be removed by child protective agencies rather than give up the relationship with their abuser. As they take the perspective of the abuser, the children are at fault — they complained about the situation, they brought the attention of authorities to the home, and they put the adult relationship at risk. Sadly, the children have now become a danger to the victim's safety. For those with Stockholm Syndrome, allowing the children to be removed from the home decreases their victim stress while providing an emotionally and physically safer environment for the children.

Perceived inability to escape

As a hostage in a bank robbery, threatened by criminals with guns, it's easy to understand the perceived inability to escape. In romantic relationships, the belief that one can't escape is also very common. Many abusive/controlling relationships feel like till-death-do-us-part relationships — locked together by mutual financial issues/assets, mutual intimate knowledge, or legal situations. Here are some common situations:

Controlling partners have increased the financial obligations/debt in the relationship to the point that neither partner can financially survive on their own. Controllers who sense their partner may be leaving will often purchase a new car, later claiming they can't pay alimony or child support due to their large car payments.

The legal ending of a relationship, especially a marital relationship, often creates significant problems. A controller who has an income that is "under the table" or maintained through legally questionable situations runs the risk of those sources of income being investigated or made public by the divorce/separation. The controller then becomes more agitated about the possible public exposure of their business arrangements than the loss of the relationship.

The controller often uses extreme threats including threatening to take the children out of state, threatening to quit their job/business rather than pay alimony/support, threatening public exposure of the victim's personal issues, or assuring the victim they will never have a peaceful life due to nonstop harassment. In severe cases, the controller may threaten an action that will undercut the victim's support such as "I'll see that you lose your job" or "I'll have your car burned".

Controllers often keep the victim locked into the

relationship with severe guilt — threatening suicide if the victim leaves. The victim hears "I'll kill myself in front of the children", "I'll set myself on fire in the front yard", or "Our children won't have a father/mother if you leave me."

In relationships with an abuser or controller, the victim has also experienced a loss of self esteem, self confidence, and psychological energy. The victim may feel "burned out" and too depressed to leave. Additionally, abusers and controllers often create a type of dependency by controlling the finances, placing cars/homes in their name, and eliminating any assets or resources the victim may use to leave. In clinical practice, things have been said like this:

"I'd leave but I can't even get money out of the savings account. I don't know the PIN number."

In teens and young adults, victims may be attracted to a controlling individual when they feel inexperienced, insecure, and overwhelmed by a change in their life situation. When parents are going through a divorce, a teen may attach to a controlling individual, feeling the controller may stabilize their life. Students at University may be attracted to controlling individuals who promise to help them survive living away from home on a University campus.

In unhealthy relationships and definitely in Stockholm Syndrome there is a daily preoccupation with "trouble". Trouble is any individual, group, situation, comment, casual glance, or cold meal that may produce a temper tantrum or verbal abuse from the controller or abuser. To survive, "trouble" is to be avoided at all costs. The victim must control situations that produce trouble. That may include avoiding family, friends, co-workers, and anyone who may create "trouble" in the abusive relationship. The victim does not hate family and friends; they are only avoiding "trouble". The victim also cleans the house, calms the children, scans the mail, avoids certain topics, and anticipates every issue of the controller or abuse in an effort to avoid "trouble". In this situation, children who are noisy become "trouble". Loved ones and friends are sources of "trouble" for the victim who is attempting to avoid verbal or physical aggression.

Stockholm Syndrome in relationships is not uncommon. Law enforcement professionals are painfully aware of the situation — making a domestic dispute one of the high-risk calls during work hours. Called by neighbors during a spousal abuse incident, the abuser is passive upon arrival of the police, only to find the abused spouse upset and threatening the officers if their abusive partner is arrested for domestic violence.

In truth, the victim knows the abuser/controller will retaliate against him/her if 1) they encourage an arrest, 2) they offer statements about the abuse/fight that are deemed disloyal by the abuser, 3) they don't bail them out of jail as quickly as possible, and 4) they don't personally apologize for the situation — as though it was their fault.

Stockholm Syndrome produces an unhealthy bond with the controller and abuser. It is the reason many victims continue to support an abuser after the relationship is over. It's also the reason they continue to see "the good side" of an abusive individual and appear sympathetic to someone who has mentally and sometimes physically abused them.

Is there something else involved?

In a short response — Yes. Throughout history, people have found themselves supporting and participating in life situations that range from abusive to bizarre. In talking to these active and willing participants in bad and bizarre situations, it is clear they have developed feelings and attitudes that support their participation. One way these feelings and thoughts are developed is known as "cognitive dissonance". As you can tell, psychologists have large words and phrases for just about everything.

"Cognitive dissonance" explains how and why people change their ideas and opinions to support situations that do not appear to be healthy, positive, or normal. In the theory, an individual seeks to reduce information or opinions that make him or her uncomfortable. When we have two sets of cognitions (knowledge, opinion, feelings, input from others, etc.) that are the opposite, the situation becomes emotionally uncomfortable. Even though we might find ourselves in a foolish or difficult situation — few want to admit that fact. Instead, we attempt to reduce the dissonance — the fact that our cognitions don't match, agree, or make sense when combined. "Cognitive dissonance" can be reduced by adding new cognitions — adding new thoughts and attitudes. Some examples:

Heavy smokers know smoking causes lung cancer and multiple health risks. To continue smoking, the smoker changes his cognitions (thoughts/feelings) such as 1) "I'm smoking less than ten years ago", 2) "I'm smoking low-tar cigarettes", 3) "Those statistics are made up by the cancer industry conspiracy", or 4) "Something's got to get you anyway." These new cognitions/attitudes allow them to keep smoking and actually begin blaming restaurants for being unfair.

You purchase a $40,000.00 sport utility vehicle that gets 3.4 kilometres a litre. (equivalent to 8 miles a gallon) You justify the expense and related issues with 1) "It's great on trips" (you take one trip per year), 2) "I can use it to haul stuff" (one coffee table in 12 months), and 3) "You can carry a lot of people in it" (95% of your trips are driver-only).

Your husband/boyfriend becomes abusive and assaultive. You can't leave due to the finances, children, or other factors. Through cognitive dissonance, you begin telling yourself "He only hits me open-handed" and "He's had a lot of stress at work."

Leon Festinger first coined the term "cognitive dissonance". He had observed a cult (1956) in which members gave up their homes, incomes, and jobs to work for the cult. This cult believed in messages from outer space that predicted the day the world would end by a flood. As cult members and firm believers, they believed they would be saved by flying saucers at the appointed time. As they gathered and waited to be taken by flying saucers at the specified time, the end-of-the-world came and went. No flood and no flying saucer.

Rather than believing they were foolish after all that personal and emotional investment — they decided their beliefs had actually saved the world from the flood and they became firmer in their beliefs after the failure of the prophecy. The moral: the more you invest (income, job, home, time, effort, etc.) the stronger your need to justify your position. If we invest $5.00 in a raffle ticket, we justify losing with "I'll get them next time". If you invest everything you have, it requires an almost unreasoning belief and unusual attitude to support and justify that investment.

Studies tell us we are more loyal and committed to something that is difficult, uncomfortable, and even humiliating. The initiation rituals of college fraternities, marine boot camp, and graduate school all produce loyal and committed individuals. Almost any ordeal creates a bonding experience. Every couple, no matter how mismatched, falls in love in the movies after going through a terrorist takeover, being stalked by a killer, being stranded on an island, or being involved in an alien abduction. Investment and an ordeal are ingredients for a strong bonding — even if the bonding is unhealthy. No one bonds or falls in love by being a member of the Car club or a music CD club. Struggling to survive on a deserted island — you bet.

Abusive relationships produce a great amount of unhealthy investment in both parties. In many cases we tend to remain and support the abusive relationship due to our investment in the relationship. Try telling a new marine that since he or she has survived boot camp, they should now enroll in the National Guard. Several types of investments keep us in the bad relationship:

Emotional investment

We've invested so many emotions, cried so much, and worried so much that we feel we must see the relationship through to the finish.

Social investment

We've got our pride. To avoid social embarrassment and uncomfortable social situations, we remain in the relationship.

Family investments

If children are present in the relationship, decisions regarding the relationship are clouded by the status and needs of the children.

Financial investment

In many cases, the controlling and abusive partner has created a complex financial situation. Many victims remain in a bad relationship, waiting for a better financial situation to develop that would make their departure and detachment easier.

Lifestyle investment

Many controlling/abusive partners use money or a lifestyle as an investment. Victims in this situation may not want to lose their current lifestyle.

Intimacy investment

We often invest emotional and sexual intimacy. Some victims have experienced a destruction of their emotional and/or sexual self-esteem in the unhealthy relationship. The abusing partner may threaten to spread rumors or tell intimate details or secrets. A type of blackmail using intimacy is often found in these situations.

In many cases, it's not simply our feelings for an individual that keep us in an unhealthy relationship — it's often the amount of investment. Relationships are complex and we often only see the tip of the iceberg in public. For this reason, the most common phrase offered by the victim in defense of their unhealthy relationship is "You just don't understand."

Combining two unhealthy conditions

The combination of "Stockholm Syndrome" and "cognitive dissonance" produces a victim who firmly believes the relationship is not only acceptable, but also desperately needed for their survival. The victim feels they would mentally collapse if the relationship ended. In long-term relationships, the victims have invested everything and placed "all their eggs in one basket". The relationship now decides their level of self-esteem, self-worth, and emotional health.

For reasons described above, the victim feels family and friends are a threat to the relationship and eventually to their personal health and existence. The more family/friends protest the controlling and abusive nature of the relationship, the more the victim develops cognitive dissonance and becomes defensive. At this point, family and friends become victims of the abusive and controlling individual.

Importantly, both Stockholm Syndrome and cognitive dissonance develop on an involuntary basis. The victim does not purposely invent this attitude. Both develop as an attempt to exist and survive in a threatening and controlling environment and relationship. They are trying to survive. Their personality is developing the feelings and thoughts needed to survive the situation and lower their emotional and physical risks. All of us have developed attitudes and feelings that help us accept and survive situations. As we have found throughout history, the more dysfunctional the situation, the more dysfunctional our adaptation and thoughts to survive.

Bottom line, my dear friend: Abuse isn't love. Love isn't abuse. If the narcissist has you thinking you can't live without them, that's Stockholm Syndrome. You needn't feel guilt or shame like the narcissist does. That's how they hold you captive as their victim. The world of pain you've been in, inflicted onto you by the narcissist or narcissists in your life can end. You have the power to end it. You have the strength to leave for good, to not turn back. Right now, you mightn't believe it, because the narcissist has had you so drained, so questioning reality, filling you with self doubt. What is there to say other than that they're good at what they do. And that's what they do. Sucking the soul out of you. That's all they have. That's all they'll ever have. You, though, my dear friend can rewrite your story. And you can do it any time at all that you wish to. Hey, you could even do it now.

Next, my dear friend, I'm going to go over the cycle of abuse, and what relates to that. As you read through it, please reflect on how this cycle has replayed in your own instance with the narcissist or narcissists in your life over and over again.

6

THE NARCISSISTIC ABUSE CYCLE

If you think about it, my dear friend, you'll recognise that there's always been an alternation between "sweetness" (never genuine) and meanness with the narcissistic abuser/s in your life. Am I right? Yes.

Let's analyse just exactly how the narcissistic cycle of abuse is actually worse than the more shall we say "standard" types of abuse. And why this is the case.

The cycle of abuse that Lenore Walker (1979) coined of tension building, acting-out, reconciliation/honeymoon, and calm is useful in most abusive relationships. However, when a narcissist is the abuser, the cycle looks different. How so? And why?

Here's the thing, my dear friend: Narcissism changes the back end of the cycle because the narcissist is constantly self centred and unwilling to admit fault. Their need to be superior, right, or in charge limits the possibility of any real reconciliation. Instead, it is frequently the abused who desperately tries for appeasement while the narcissist plays the victim. This switchback tactic emboldens the narcissistic behavior even more, further convincing them of their faultlessness. Any threat to their authority repeats the cycle again. If you as the victim continue in this codependent state, it will go over and over again indefinitely.

In a nutshell, here are the four narcissistic cycles of abuse:

Narcissist feels threatened:

An upsetting event occurs and the narcissist feels threatened. It could be rejection of sex, disapproval at work, embarrassment in a social setting, jealousy of other's success, or feelings of abandonment, neglect, or disrespect. The abused, aware of the potential threat, becomes nervous. They know something is about to happen and begin to walk on eggshells around the narcissist. Most narcissists repeatedly get upset over the same underlying issues whether the issue is real or imagined. They also have a tendency to obsess over the threat over and over.

Narcissist abuses others:

The narcissist engages in some sort of abusive behavior. The abuse can be physical, mental, verbal, sexual, financial, spiritual or emotional. The abuse is customized to intimidate the abused in an area of weakness especially if that area is one of strength for the narcissist. The abuse can last for a few short minutes or as long as several hours. Sometimes a combination of two types of abuse is used. For instance, a narcissist may begin with verbal belittling to wear out the abused. Followed by projection of their lying about an event onto the abused. Finally tired of the assault, the abused defensively fights back.

Narcissist becomes the victim:

This is when the switchback occurs. The narcissist uses the abused behavior as further evidence that they are the ones being abused. The narcissist believes their own twisted victimization by bringing up past defensive behaviors that the abused has done as if the abused initiated the abuse. Because the abused has feelings of remorse and guilt, they accept this warped perception and try to rescue the narcissist. This might include giving into what the narcissist wants, accepting unnecessary responsibility, placating the narcissist to keep the peace, and agreeing to the narcissistic lies.

Narcissist feels empowered:

Once the abused have given in or up, the narcissist feels empowered. This is all the justification the narcissist needs to demonstrate their rightness or superiority. The abused has unknowingly fed the narcissistic ego and only to make it stronger and bolder than before. But every narcissist has an Achilles heel and the power they feel now will only last till the next threat to their ego appears.

Once the narcissistic cycle of abuse is understood, the abused can escape the cycle at any point. Begin by coming up with strategies for future confrontations, know the limitations of the abused, and have an escape plan in place. This cycle does not need to continue forward.

Some terms in relation to this narcissistic cycle of abuse that it's vital you understand are as follows, my dear friend:

"Hoovering":

Basically, hoovering is a narcissist sucking the life out of you. It might have been some time since the narcissist in your life has contacted you. It could be a week, a month, months, even years. Then, suddenly out of the blue, they contact you. It seemed that you were safe from their manipulation, as you'd received nothing from them other than the silent treatment.

So, hoovering is a technique narcissists use to suck their

victims back into a relationship with them. As always, there's an agenda. Never is there not an agenda on their part. Yes, hoovering is named after the Hoover vacuum cleaner. Even more appropriate, because the hooverer narcissist is treating you like dirt. Yes, dirt.

This is when your narcissist or narcissists are being seemingly "sweet" to you. Do not fall for it. Under any circumstances. It's simply to reel you in again, so they can devaluate you faster and faster each and every time. So, say for example, as happened with me, NPD biological mother, after I had gone no contact with her, and changed my mobile phone number, along with any of my siblings who had no right to contact me when they only ever pretty much did so to ask something from me in regards to NPD mother can no longer contact me.

And although I asked my wife to change her mobile number too, and not let it be known to any of my biological family members, she wouldn't. So, long story short: Only my eldest brother and sibling can contact me through my wife. At least, it's not direct. He's actually the only one I would want to have any contact with anyway.

So, on a couple of instances since having gone no contact with NPD biological mother, I have been in a large crowd at a couple of events where my eldest brother's wife has been. I was at these events with both my wife and daughter. In one instance, my eldest brother was with his wife. Now, they are the third party NPD biological mother is using to attempt to "hoover" me through. Lovely people. Who have emotionally stable fully grown adult children because of emotionally healthy parenting with them. And proper boundaries. Despite how lovely they are, I saw it for what it was. An attempt for NPD biological mother to "hoover" me. The difference now being that my eyes were now wide open, and I was fully healed from the approximately forty odd years of damage she had caused to me previously. I no longer had any codependent, "Stockholm Syndrome" emotional bond or connection with or to her. And I know that I never will. And I'm totally fine and at peace with that.

So, on both of these occasions, what does my lovely sister in law do but convey my NPD biological mother's "love" being sent, and on one of those instances, her apologies for not being able to be there herself. As if I even cared. I was extremely happy with how I dealt with that on both occasions. A far cry to all of my life prior to it.

On the occasion when my eldest brother was also there, NPD biological mother had requested a family photo be taken. Yes, let's play happy families. Whilst in my mind, I roll my eyes. Whatever. Because I know exactly what she's doing. I also know that she thinks I am a mere extension of her, as she always has thought. Not a separate person with free will to do as I please. However, that's what I am now doing. Not buying into any of that rubbish. Not allowing any of them to control me beyond my boundaries. Living my life, on my terms. With my own family, the one I created.

Quick recap on the why of their hoovering you: Narcissists need the energy of being adored, and who better to suck that energy than someone they decide is still vulnerable to them? As emotional vampires, they have no problem destroying you to get their needs met. They can be at a low point in their life and may need a quick-fix, (Let's face it, why wouldn't they be at a low point? After all, it's practically their entire existence), so they look for the easiest and quickest source: you.

The bitter truth is that they have no intention of

everything working out and giving you a happily-ever-after. For whatever reason, things aren't going the hooverer's way — maybe the person they dumped you for isn't working out or did something that annoyed them; he's getting ready to dump her or he might need something you have, like money, a car or sex.

I was so enmeshed for so long, my dear friend. But when I finally woke up, how I did wake up. That's why we are from that point on no longer vulnerable to them. Once you get some self worth, and know what you're worth, you won't accept any less. And that's healthy. Now, here's some more information on what they'll do when they're hoovering:

1. They send you messages pretending nothing happened.

One day with no warning you get a message that says, "Hey stranger, long time no talk" or, "What's up?" Do not engage.

2. They use the pretext of a special occasion to make contact.

Just translate "Happy Anniversary" or "Happy New Year" to mean "I need some attention." Do not engage.

3. They ask you random questions.

"What was the name of the sushi restaurant we went to in …?" Feel free to answer any way you want, but they don't really want to know the answer; they just want to get you to focus on them. If possible, dear friend, I suggest you simply shrug as if you don't know. Just be prepared for more of a barrage. If you can avoid engaging, by all means do so.

4. They make a fake gesture of caring.

What I mentioned via a third party with my NPD biological mother is a perfect instance of precisely this. "I was thinking about you" means "I was thinking about me" and "how I can use you to distract myself." Don't fall for it, and, to the extent possible, do not engage.

5. They bring your kids into it.

"I know you hate me, but please tell Nate to score a goal for me." Don't fall for it. Do not engage. (However, if you feel the need to vomit or put your fingers down your throat, please do so. You are, after all, only human.)

6. They become your social director.

"Hey, want to catch up on some of the Oscar-nominated films with me?" No, I absolutely don't. Once again, do not engage.

7. They praise you.

"I read your piece on the philosophy of Beyonce Knowles and I was riveted. Your writing speaks to me." Yeah, well, listen closely because it's telling you to leave me the heck alone. Once more, do not engage.

8. They call you to say something bogus.

Any hooverer knows that it's very difficult to resist when someone reaches out during a crisis. But there's no need to be concerned — there's no aunt with cancer and the hooverer isn't concerned about a mole on his left shoulder. They're simply using every trick in the handbook. Do not engage.

9. They "accidentally" call or text you.

Who says narcissists can't be evil geniuses? A mistake call can deliver a whole lot of pain with a few strokes. If you get a "See you in ten minutes. Love you" text, this is supposedly for his current girlfriend but is sent as a stab in the heart. Then there's the "Vicki called and said Grant is in the hospital. Call him right away" text, so that you'll feel compelled to call the hooverer. Under no circumstance should you fall for this. Do not engage.

10. They play the guilt card.

This includes the "I'll go to AA if you come back" or "I might do something harmful to myself if you don't respond" texts. The narcissist manipulator knows that it's very difficult to say no to something when someone's life is in the balance. Do this like a champ, dear friend. Do not engage.

11. They accuse you of something.

"Did you just call me?" or "Was that you driving past my house just now?" No one likes to be accused of hoovering someone, but the hooverer is just trying to get you to respond. Absolutely positively do not engage.

12. They make false accusations.

"Stop stalking me," they text you as you shake your head in confusion. What? Who's stalking who? You should be able to see this clearly for what it is: An attempt to get you to defend yourself, explain yourself. Get enmeshed in their drawing you in. Stick to your guns, dear friend. There's nothing to explain to a narcissist when they don't matter any more. When you've learnt all about their sordid little table of tricks. In case it isn't obvious by now, do not engage.

It's tempting when you finally hear the things you've wanted to hear since you got dumped, and you think this will help heal the pain. But no, it will do just the opposite. The hooverer doesn't really care about you because you're only a part of their sick game. Choose not to play. Do not engage.

People with personality disorders like narcissism don't have lasting relationships, and they don't feel love for anybody but themselves. The reason they're hoovering you is one hundred percent for themselves — you aren't even in the equation.

"Ghosting":

Ghosting is well documented in the mental health world as being a tactic emotional abusers use, (aka your narcissist/s) to try and control and damage the self esteem of those people they are in a relationship with. The ironic thing is with the narcissist/s in your life, once you've reached a point of having had enough of them, and having woken up to them, you honestly don't care if they contact you anyway. Basically, ghosting is when your narcissist/s go quiet on their end. You don't hear from them. In effect, it's a narcissist dishing out to you their silent treatment. Can I just say enjoy the silence! Once you no longer have any connection to them, it's no longer even going to work with you.

Here's a list of some reasons as to why your narcissist/s would use ghosting on you:

They are an emotional toddler who lacks communication skills. Don't forget that your narcissist/s might want to use you for supply in the future at any given time. Aka hoovering.

They are incredibly self centred, and only see life from their view point.

They have mental health issues: i.e. being a narcissist, sociopath or psychopath.

"Gaslighting":

Inspired by the 1940 and 1944 films "Gas Light," where a husband systematically manipulates his wife in order to make her feel crazy, the term "Gaslighting" is now commonly used to describe behavior that is inherently manipulative.

Gaslighting, at its core, is a form of emotional abuse that slowly eats away at your ability to make judgments. Essentially, a gaslighter spins their negative, harmful or destructive words and actions in their favor, deflecting the blame for their abusive deeds and pointing the finger at you. This is often done by making you feel "overly sensitive," "paranoid," "mentally unstable," "silly," "unhinged," and many other sensations which cause you to doubt yourself. Commonly adopted by psychopathic, sociopathic and narcissistic types of people, gaslighting tends to eat away at you slowly until you realize that you're a shell of the former person you were.

Let's take a look at some examples of gaslighting:

In a family scenario: Peter's father is an angry, bitter man. Every day Peter is afraid to "tip the balance" of his father's mood because he often bursts out in fits of rage calling Peter a "poophead" and a "worthless little loser," among many other hurtful names. When Peter confronts his father about this aggressive name calling, Peter's father laughs and tells him "to stop being so sensitive."

In a relationship scenario: Kate has been married for 5 years and has two small children with her husband Stewart. For the past few months Kate has been trying to establish a small art shop, but when she asks for her husband's assistance his mood darkens: "I can't believe you're spending so much time on this shop—don't you care about me—don't you care about your kids? You're supposed to be mothering them," he exclaims. Kate is shocked, "But I just wanted you to help me with setting up the store. And I haven't been neglecting anyone."
Stewart comes up very close to Kate's face: "You see. Now you're denying it. When I married you I thought you'd be there for your family. I should just take the kids and go already." Stewart storms off. Later, when Kate sits down to talk with Stewart about his threat, Stewart says, "Honey, you know you were over reacting, and you know that you've been obsessing over this shop too much. That makes the rest of us feel very ignored and excluded,
I hope you understand that."

An at work scenario: Bianca has been working in her department for the past five years when she is given a promotion to migrate to another level of the company that pays a higher salary. However, Bianca has been given a trial period to determine whether she is capable of fulfilling her duties or not. Nervously, she meets with her new supervisor, Tracy. At first, Bianca likes her supervisor and fulfills all of her tasks on time. However, her supervisor begins to ask her to do belittling chores and favors here and there with increasing frequency. While Bianca is fine with helping out, she finds that Tracy is becoming more and more demanding. Finally, as Bianca's work piles up to an unbearable level, she tells Tracy that she needs to focus on completing her work, but she can help another time.

Later, in a staff meeting, Tracy introduces Bianca to everyone and says, "Although she's not keeping up with us yet, I'm sure she'll learn to embody our hard-working ethics soon." Immediately, Bianca blushes and feels publicly insulted and humiliated, fearing for the security of her new job. Later when Bianca asks her supervisor why she thinks that "she is not embodying their hard working ethic," her supervisor says: "I think you misunderstood me. I just said that you're not used to our pace of work so that other people can help you out." From then on Bianca accepts all extra demands and chores, no matter how much work she has, or how demeaning the tasks are.

Gaslighting is so harmful because it promotes anxiety, depression, and with enough frequency in our lives, can sometimes trigger nervous breakdowns. So the question now is: are you being gaslighted? How can you know whether you're experiencing this subtle form of manipulation in your life? Review the following tell-tale signs:

Something is "off" about your friend, partner, son, daughter, mother, father, sister, brother, colleagues, boss, or other person in your life … but you can't quite explain or pinpoint what.

You frequently second guess your ability to remember the details of past events leaving you psychologically powerless.

You feel confused and disorientated.

You feel threatened and on edge around this person, but you don't know why.

You feel the need to apologize all the time for what you do or who you are.

You never quite feel "good enough" and try to live up to the expectations and demands of others, even if they are unreasonable or harm you in some way.

You feel like there's something fundamentally wrong with you, e.g. you're neurotic or are "losing it."

You feel like you're constantly overreacting or are "too sensitive."

You feel isolated, hopeless, misunderstood and depressed.

You find it hard to trust your own judgment, and given a choice, you choose to believe the judgment of the abuser.

You feel scared and as though "something is terribly wrong," but you don't know what or why.

You find it hard to make decisions because you distrust yourself.

You feel as though you're a much weaker version of yourself, and you were much more strong and confident in the past.

You feel guilty for not feeling happy like you used to.

You've become afraid of "speaking up" or expressing your emotions, so you stay silent instead.

Gaslighters use a variety of subtle techniques to undermine your reality and portray you as the disturbed and messed up one. These include, for example:

Discrediting you by making other people think that

you're crazy, irrational or unstable. Using a mask of confidence, assertiveness, and/or fake compassion to make you believe that you "have it all wrong." Therefore, eventually, you begin to doubt yourself and believe their version of past events.

Changing the subject. The gaslighter may divert the topic by asking another question, or making a statement usually directed at your thoughts, e.g. "You're imagining things—that never happened." "No, you're wrong, you didn't remember right." "Is that another crazy idea you got from your (family member/friend)?"

Minimizing. By trivializing how you feel and what you think, the gaslighter gains more and more power over you, e.g. "Why are you being so sensitive?" "You don't need to get angry over a little thing like that!" "I was just joking around, why are you taking things so seriously?"

Denial and avoidance. By refusing to acknowledge your feelings and thoughts, the gaslighter causes you to doubt yourself more and more. For example, "I don't remember that, you must have dreamt it!" "You're lying, I never said that." "I don't know what you're talking about, you're changing the subject."

Twisting and reframing. When the gaslighter confidently and subtly twists and reframes what was said or done in their favor, they can cause you to second-guess yourself—especially when paired with fake compassion, making you feel as though you are "unstable," "irrational," and so forth. For example, "I didn't say that, I said ______" "I didn't beat you up Harold, I just gave you a smack around the head—that's what all good fathers do." "If you remember correctly, I was actually trying to help you."

Gaslighting causes us to doubt our own memories,

perceptions, and judgments, throwing us emotionally and psychologically off balance. If you feel as though your self-esteem, confidence, and independence has withered under the flame of gaslighting you are not alone … and there certainly is hope.

Almost all of us, including myself, have experienced one form of gaslighting or another throughout life. The problems arise when gaslighting is a frequent shadow that trails behind our relationships and partnerships. The good news is that knowledge and awareness is the first step to healing your life and rebuilding the strong, perceptive person you are. And you have already taken it.

While it is true that in some situations we genuinely might be overreacting, or might genuinely be exhibiting irrational behavior, it is also important for you to listen to your instinct or intuition. Do you have a heavy feeling in the pit of your stomach? Do you feel weighed down and oppressed? Do you feel depressed? These are signs that you have unconsciously picked up on deception and "foul play." While we can consciously be fooled, unconsciously we can't, and often we will have a lingering feeling that "something just isn't right." Make sure that you listen to this feeling and seek help, either professionally (life coach) or socially (i.e. a trusted group of friends or a support network).

In summary, here are some ways to support yourself in the face of gaslighting:

Firstly clarify to yourself how, when and who (your narcissist/s) is gaslighting you. Think about what ways they make you feel unhinged and like you're losing it. Write down whatever you can think of. You must be able to confirm that you're being gaslighted before you can move on with your life. Look up online other people's experiences. In effect, it's helpful to "compare notes", my dear friend.

Pay attention to the signs of being gaslighted, like feeling confused, belittled, "crazy" or manipulated. Take a deep breath, clear your mind, and centre yourself. Set aside regular time for grounding each day through a mindfulness practice. These techniques will help you to stay objective even in difficult circumstances. They will also help you to neutralize the former reactiveness to your narcissist/s. Thus, you'll be taking back your power, along with making progress.

If you have to bide some time in your relationship with your narcissist/s, think about ways to minimize interaction with them until you feel grounded and confident. Shift your perspective from being a victim to being a warrior/winner or whatever word feels the most empowering. You don't have to remain a victim for the rest of your life, and by reclaiming your personal power, you'll also be able to help others in similar circumstances. In time. Let's get you healed, and strong first. That's priority.

7

WAYS TO STOP THE ABUSE
&
THE WOUNDS YOU NEED TO HEAL

To be forewarned is to be forearmed. What I mean is that you need some arsenal to get the message across to the narcissist/s in your life that you no longer fear them or what they think or say. If you don't as yet feel up to replying at all to your narcissist/s, that's okay. Walking away from them when they start is another way of sending the message out that you aren't invested or interested in buying into their rubbish any longer. The main thing is consistency, my dear friend. You simply need to be consistent in not reacting to them any longer. No longer are you going to be either a snack or meal for them. Starve the narcissistic beast.

I know from experience with my NPD mother that she got more desperate once she realized I was no longer invested or interested in engaging with her. So what did she then do? She pulled out all the stops to get narcissistic supply from me. But failed. Of course, since this time, I have gone no contact with her. Not that that's stopped her from hoovering through others, as I have mentioned examples of. But, the point is this: I no longer care. There's nothing to say. There's nothing to do other than to move on with my life. This is where you need to get to. And past the anger that is part of the healing.

With that in mind, here are some phrases for you to practice in your mind before perhaps using them on the narcissist/s in your life. All of these phrases will disarm your toxic narcissist/s. And send the message you want them to hear loud and clear: You are no longer willing to allow your fear of what they think to control you. Powerful stuff.

To get you in the right frame of mind for these, bear this in mind: We don't have the right or the power to change someone else's reality. Yes, even narcissists. This is different to how you have thought previously. You used to constantly feed right into it, correct? No more. No longer, my dear friend. There's no need to get upset with anyone's faulty perception of you.

Phrase number one: "I am sorry you feel that way." Don't forget, your narcissist/s think they know everything. Why you did this. Why you did that. And let's face it. We both know that they're twisting it totally around. Previously, you would have fallen for this bait. You would have gotten all enmeshed and emotional to explain yourself. Can you imagine the difference when you use this phrase instead? If you more or less simply shrug it off? Game changer? You bet.

The former dynamic is completely gone. You are disentangling yourself from that dynamic now. Therefore, their attempt to engage you is going nowhere fast. And how good would you now feel? Precisely. You've taken your power back. Whilst simultaneously having taken their power away.

Phrase number two: "I can accept your faulty perception of me." Ouch. Don't you just love it? How awesome is it? Because you are acknowledging that they have this odd perception of you. Not only that, you can accept it. You're fine with it. Situation diffused. Basically, you are saying you are comfortable in your own skin. They can't pierce that.

You are no longer engaging. If they can't engage you, then it's game over for them.

This phrase also lets them know in no uncertain terms that you will no longer be manipulated by them. That you've severed any emotional cords you formerly had. Does this take more strength? You bet. Totally does. Whatever the narcissist thinks or feels is totally okay with you. Besides, you now are aware that it's not worth wasting your energy on an emotional toddler. And that is exactly what you're dealing with. Nothing more. Nothing less.

Phrase number three: "I have no right to control how you see me." Yes, this is very similar to the previous phrase. However, there's one key difference, and that is this: You acknowledge that they see you in a way that you don't agree with, like the previous phrase, but, you're also saying that they are allowed to do so. That they are permitted to see you in absolutely any way whatsoever that they please. You think that'll disarm them? Of course it will.

Because what you are now in effect telling the narcissist is that you are no longer interested in engaging in this warfare with them. In other words, they can gaslight you, but you are simply no longer going to go there again. You are telling them that you are done with these shenanigans.

Phrase number four: "I guess I have to accept how you feel." This communicates to the narcissist that you accept who they are. Also that you allow them to be who they are. When you transmit this to the narcissist, what's the message you are sending them? That suddenly you are no longer willing to play the game. That you can accept how they feel. Remember, for the narcissist, feelings are facts. Now, if it's fact to them, what's the point in engaging into that dynamic? There is no point. And so your message to them is basically this:

Whatever. It is what it is. No engagement on your part.

The fifth and final phrase is this: "Your anger is not my responsibility." In case you'd forgot, the narcissist is completely and utterly full of anger. Anger lurks in them at any given moment, waiting to be unleashed. On you. Or whoever. The thing is now: It needn't be you. Can you heal them? Nope. Can they heal themselves? It's highly unlikely. Most probably not. Ever.

So, how does this phrase work? Well, remember that you most likely are an empathetic person. In fact, I hazard a guess to say you simply have to be. Anyone a narcissist attracts will be empathetic. They're drawn to them like a moth to a flame. You might have even wanted to fix them. Make them your responsibility. This happens when an empathetic person is in a state of codependency: seeking validation from outside of themself. Seeking approval from others. People pleasing.

In the relationship between a narcissist and a codependent, empathetic person both are focused on one person: The narcissist. The narcissist because in their warped disordered mind: They are the only one who matters. The codependent, empathetic person because of looking outside of themselves continually for approval. At whatever cost. And with the narcissist, it comes at a great cost. As you have already personally experienced.

What's the message you are sending to the narcissist, by letting them know that their anger is not your responsibility? Bear in mind, that they already know that as empaths, we dislike when people get angry. That's why they get loud. They've figured that out. So, can you imagine when they're doing this, what effect you saying their anger is not your responsibility would have on them? You didn't shut down, as you previously did when they went on their tirade. They no longer have this control over you. No longer will you be intimidated by them. You won't be manipulated any longer. You won't engage with them any longer. You no longer allow the previous fear you had of them to control you. Can you see how well that would work, my dear friend?

As I mentioned, if you need to practice these phrases repeatedly in your mind prior to using them with your narcissist/s, by all means do so. Sometimes, simply hanging up on them if it's over the phone is one way of sending the message to them. Or saying, "No. I'm not doing this," and then hang up on them. Or, if it's in person, leave the area where they are. However, you need to be confident. Not passive. And definitely not pleading. Unwavering. Otherwise, they'll sniff your vulnerability, and you are back to where you were with them previously.

The mistake we codependent empaths have previously made is this: Attempting to appeal to an empathy that simply isn't there. The narcissist could be termed as empathy deficient. Once you have your head around that, it changes things for you. You won't keep banging your head on the narcissistic brick wall. Expecting them to care. Unless there's something in it for them, they simply won't. Always there needs to be an egoic payoff for them in it.

Another crucial thing for you to bear in mind is this: Everything that comes out of their mouth is lies. If you can remember that, you will no longer engage with them. You want to neutralise the situation. If you can't go no contact with them yet, neutralisation is what you need to do. Disengage. You'll notice you are no longer bothered by what formerly caused you to react impulsively. It's kind of like you're rolling your eyes in your head. At the narcissist.

Like really? Well, okay then. Whatever. And such a positive move forward for you, my dear friend. Progress.

Whilst it may not be possible for you to go no contact yet, going "grey rock" as it's termed will serve you well in the following ways:

It allows you to reduce the amount of toxic behaviour from the narcissist/s.

It enables you to better protect or shield yourself from the psychological damage their abusive words and behaviour may otherwise have on you.

Basically, what this method entails is some behavioural choices that you will use in response to the narcissist/s' abusive, manipulating behaviour.

Much like a grey rock, you will be keeping your "head down", simply blending into the environment. Your intention is to starve the narcissist/s in your life of any type of reward, supply or emotional responses. How? By remaining in a neutral state, irrespective of how they behave. From experience with my own NPD mother, I know that this works well.

What is going to be the effect of this change on your part? The narcissist/s in your life will not find their interactions with you anywhere near as stimulating as they previously did. Meaning that they will focus their time and energy on whoever else will serve them better so as to get their needs met.

You will do as follows from this point on with them:

Speak in a voice devoid of emotion. With little to no inflections. Yes, be a robot.

Give them only concise, matter of fact answers to any questions. You will not elaborate. I repeat: you will not elaborate.

Keep on only boring, surface topics if you absolutely have to engage in conversation with them.

When they use insults on you, you will not either engage or defend yourself from these.

Use very little or no eye contact with them. Only if absolutely necessary will you have any eye contact.

Show no interest in the narcissist/s dramatic stories. (Some of which you may likely have heard countless times in the past on repeat)

Definitely, under no circumstances whatsoever, do not give out to them any personal information. Why? So that you cut off any ideas that may be used by them against you so as to hurt you further.

It's important to realise that consistency with doing these things is key. It's going to take time to reprogram the narcissistic abuser/s in your life. Therefore, you must absolutely commit to acting this way so that your abuser will eventually become bored with it. My dear friend, can you do this? Yes, you can.

As I mentioned in the case with my own NPD mother, yes, they will try harder with you. It's sheer desperation. Remember, you are dealing with an emotional child. How else would you expect them to act? Nonetheless, when this happens, don't be railroaded by it or them. Because this is usually right before they become bored.

I feel that now would be a good time to go over the

cycle of narcissistic abuse some more. There's the initial "seemingly nice" stage, where the narcissist draws you in. Yes, it's fake. Yes, it's insincere. Yes, they will flatter you. This stage is often referred to as "love bombing". They make your head spin. And fast. You can get swept up in the enthrallment of it, the seeming appreciation of you and all that you are. Beware. The proverbial rug can be ripped out from under you by the narcissist at any given time, and you've likely already been through this.

Basically, the initial stage of the cycle, the "love bombing" can be termed the "Idealization" part of the abuse cycle. The narcissist seems to idolise you during this stage. Therefore, this stage could also be termed as the "Idolisation" phase.

"Idealization": This stage is when the narcissist/s in your life treat you like a new shiny toy. Yes, toy. Keep that in mind, because toys can be discarded by children, usually without warning, so it's an apt parallel analogy given the emotional toddlerhood of the narcissist. And there will be a discard of you.

So, you are familiar with infatuation? Fake love? That's what this stage is on the part of the narcissist. And like infatuation, you are during this stage an obsession for the narcissist. During this phase, you are actually helping the narcissist to self medicate. Sad, but true, my dear friend.

You see, the narcissist simply cannot bear to be left alone with themselves. Because all they have when alone are inner feelings of the negative kind: emptiness, aloneness, deficiency, defectiveness. These feelings, like acid, gnaw away at them. This is because the narcissist has no stable inner self. That being so, gaining attention and approval is the only way in which they can get any sense of self. From an outside source. A source outside of themselves.

Otherwise, the narcissist is left with their highly insecure ego. That feels worthless and dead without attention. As already mentioned, any attention is better than none at all. This is, after all, an adult child with inner wounds that are unhealed. At this stage, you'll be placed on a pedestal. You may be compared (especially if this is a romantic relationship) to previous supply (former flames, spouse or partners). You will, of course, be so much better than anyone prior to you. At this point, you are giving your narcissist a "high". Because, at this moment, they are having magical, childlike thinking. And you are the shiny, newest toy. Wow. You are so amazing. You are so attractive. You are so special. For now.

The greater the supply to the narcissist is perceived to be by them, the better they feel. This is bound to come crashing down soon enough. Because it's unrealistic. Because it's unsustainable. Because they have blown up in their belief, just how awesome the supply is. It's rose coloured glasses on steroids.

You, as the narcissists victim/supply, may be presented with gifts, along with thoughtful special acts. Your ego will be stroked. You'll be made to feel good for who you are. Because you are codependent, and have tended to undervalue yourself, as opposed to knowing your worth, is it any wonder you are bound to feel "finally appreciated" by the narcissist? And as if you feel more whole and in love with yourself? Someone's paid attention. Someone's taken notice. And that feels good. It's as if you've finally found your bestest friend ever.

During this phase, you have been open and trusting with the narcissist. As a result, you have placed your emotional wellbeing and life in the hands of the narcissist. Your vulnerability has basically been exploited by the narcissist, without your awareness. They sniffed you out whilst your defences were cast aside. Now comes the next phase: Devaluation.

"Devaluation": This phase starts for at least some part of the "idealisation" phase. However, due to you having been swept away and caught up in the heady rush of the "idealisation" phase, you haven't necessarily picked up on the vagueish initial warning signs. The initial red flags.

This phase is when those red flags become undeniable. When that flattery on the part of the narcissist, those declarations that you were valued in a special, unique way are revealed to have never been real. Let that sink in: That they were not at any stage real. And so they are now revealed as not having been anything other than lies. They'll show this by both words and actions. Yes, the big reveal has come during this phase. The mask comes off to the beast lurking beneath. That the facts always have been that they despise you, that they want to destroy you, that they clearly hate you. It's nothing short of horrible, given the speed of the change from the initial idealisation of you. And so you're left reeling.

The actions that show the true self, rather than the false self ego that had previously "hooked" you in are of the nature that follows:

Showing that they have no concern for you at all despite you being in what could be a situation that is potentially threatening.

They're unavailable when you are either sick, distressed or in need.

They'll play "tit for tat" whenever you are in need.

They'll be angered when you are in need.

They have an STD but don't tell you, yet still have sex with you.

You are going to feel not right about these different and seemingly odd behaviours from them, given how they were acting different previously. They've now proved that they care nothing about your wellbeing and your actual self. Your physical health or even your very life might even be at stake. After this phase comes the final phase of narcissistic abuse: The Discard.

"Discard": This happens upon your usefulness to the narcissist having reached it's end. Due to the fact that you were only ever in the narcissist's life to provide "attention". Simply put, my dear friend, that's the energy that allows the narcissist to self regulate their fragile and precarious false self ego. It's a bitter pill to swallow, I know. All the same, it still trumps living in denial. And with an unconscious contract with the narcissist along the lines of "If I give, give, give, you'll meet my needs. I can't express my needs, but you'll meet them if I give enough."

So, because the "attention" you are providing is no longer good enough quality for the narcissist anymore, (likely they've drained you, or you're reeling as the mask comes off savagely, maybe a combination of both) or you have threatened the false self ego in a way that undermines the narcissist's fabricated image, they may cease all investment in you and begin the quest to secure another source of better grade narcissistic supply. Are you breathing a sigh of relief? You should be.

At this point, what may also have happened is that a better narcissistic supply option has presented, and the narcissist suddenly removed themselves to enmesh with the "newest shiniest toy". Yes, you are replaceable. Yes, just like that. No, you are not meant to care that they've done this to you. Come on. You're a plaything. They're done with you. Or at least for the time being.

If you have incited the narcissist's wrath (as many people do simply by trying to defend their own rights) the narcissist may discard you, turn you into "the enemy" and set out to tear your life apart piece by piece. (Even from some distance away, when I called my NPD brother out on social media for being jealous of me, I felt his wrath. I recall being shocked at the time at how swift and brutal the response was. I had no idea at that time what I was dealing with. It had the effect of "silencing" me. It shook me to the core.)

The discard phase is the last part of the cycle. However, it may not be the end of the relationship. The narcissist may not discard permanently. The facts are that many often don't, and that depends largely on what the person who has been discarded has running as painful insecurities (gaps). This is why you have to do the inner work, my dear friend. So that you heal and eliminate those insecurities. Otherwise, you are still a sitting duck. A target for the narcissist. Any gaps in you, any insecurities, they will use against you. You will simply be more wounded. I don't think you deserve that. In fact, I know that you don't.

If a narcissist discards you and knows that letting go and abandoning you hurts you intensely, then a narcissist may be very likely to stay away. They're getting the narcissistic supply (satisfaction) that this is really hurting you. Yes, it's sick. Yes, it's okay to be angry about this. It's better still if you use that anger to heal and thrive. Without the narcissist/s in your life.

A narcissist knowing that someone else is in severe

emotional pain over them, gains a great deal of significance. It goes like this, "If I can affect someone powerfully emotionally, that confirms how special I am."

What it is really doing is confirming to the narcissistic that he or she exists. Period. Reiterating, the narcissist is the walking "empty soul" that is not real and full. Hence, why the temporary highs of feeling "valid" are greatly valued and sought after.

So, especially, if the narcissist is receiving feedback that you are severely affected by their departure, and you try to contact or make contact with others who know the narcissist, stalk or do the things that the narcissist knows about will you grant them that. They will love to hear how hurt you are.

But wait. Here's the worst. Even if you are just energetically emotionally hurt without creating any physical evidence, then still at a subconscious level the narcissist feels it, remains "fed" and will keep doing whatever provides "the feed". Which in this instance is
keeping away.

Sometimes this may be something that puzzles you, though: "Why is the narcissist not hoovering? Why are they keeping away from me?"

I'll answer that shortly. However, first, my dear friend, please consider this: The very fact that so many people are asking, means that they have not come to terms with it and are playing out their young wounds (trauma attachment) of feeling unlovable, not important, not valued and abandoned, that are still deep wounds from childhood. Yes, many of us either still are or have previously been wounded children in adult bodies. Myself included.

Now, the positive we don't realise at the point we ask this question is this: The narcissist, in this case, is actually smashing our greatest emotional wounds open. And yes, it does hurt like crazy. But why is it that they are able to do precisely this? It's so that finally the submerged subconscious can emerge, (our unconscious contract with the narcissist) become conscious, and be healed.

I hear you ask: How can we do that? We do it only when we stop trying to force the narcissist to be responsible for healing these wounds. Truly, how can they do that? When they're constantly running from any responsibility and accountability? When we instead break away from them, and go inwards, (we've previously been going outwards: i.e. people pleasing, seeking approval and validation from others) self partner, meet ourselves and heal them ourselves, then true healing occurs. And from that point on, it gets better and better.

To conclude this chapter, from time to time I notice people "complaining" that we (codependents, empaths) are the ones who have to change. Why us? (Victim mentality right there) Simply explained, because we can. We have self reflection. We have the ability to heal. The narcissist/s in our lives don't. It truly appears that they are irrepairably damaged.

If you have read this far, if you have gotten this book, that means you can repair all of your damage. Our brains, along with all the cells in our bodies are like plastic, in a sense. We can create new pathways with these. New neural pathways. I know from personal experience. Positive reinforcements, positive affirmations reprogram us. If you can continue daily to do positive affirmations for a period of twenty one to sixty or so days, (roughly three weeks to two months) you won't be the same person you were before. I guarantee it. And when all that negative junk, that programming from your younger years is gone, it's beyond awesome.

My dear friend, there is genuinely such a vast chasm between who I am now to who I was not that long ago. Who I was for the first over forty years of my life. I want the same for you. Us beautiful souls deserve it. After all we've been though. I know for so long I really couldn't see the light at the end of the tunnel. Yes, I was seemingly trapped in a perpetual long, dark tunnel. Until I went inwards, rather than outwards. Until I showed all that love, empathy, compassion, and more to myself, as opposed to those who abused that, drained me of it, and for what? I'll allow you to answer that question in your own mind.

In the next chapter, I am going to go over some narcissist family dynamics. This may or may not apply to you personally. I appreciate and understand that. However, I do think that the more insights you gain, the better off you are to see in others what you well may have missed for oh so long. Perhaps even your lifetime up until now.

You see, when we begin to learn some things related to narcissism, we get excited. However, the self love recovery process ia a process. And just when you think that you may know a lot, you learn more. I've personally had some people get excited that they know something about narcissists. Then swiftly label someone as NPD. However, I've been able to say to such people that that person may be exhibiting some narcissistic traits, but not be narcissistic personality disordered. (This is usually when I have had interaction with that person myself at some point) Because, quite bluntly, let's face it: labelling someone incorrectly as NPD isn't what this is actually about.

You simply know how you feel around and with an NPD person. And, if you are really in tune with yourself, you may realise you didn't feel that way around that person that someone has labelled as NPD. That has been my experience. The person may have shown some genuine feeling. The person may have done something without expecting anything back. Without an egoic payoff. In your self love recovery journey, the more knowledge you gain, the more, like myself, you will know. To be able to say yes or no to someone being NPD. Oh, and the really cool thing is that you will stop attracting narcissists to you. Because there will no longer be any vulnerable emotional wounds for them to break open. Cool, huh?

8

ROLES & DYNAMICS IN NARCISSISTIC FAMILIES EXPLAINED

The narcissistic family is ruled by the narcissistic partner or spouse parent. In my own NPD ruled mess of a "family", my NPD mother ruled the roost. My codependent enabling father I see now felt stuck. I also see that he felt angry at times, although a relatively placid personality prior to dementia.

What I remember is my father bailing out my two older brothers closest in age to me quite a lot. Both are alcoholics. The older one is fourteen years older than me. I have no recollection of any of my older siblings living at home, except for my NPD brother closest in age to me. I remember NPD mother pouring down the sink contents of alcohol bottles she'd found of my NPD brother. Seriously, it was a madhouse, when I reflect.

My brother fourteen years older than me hasn't had any kind of a relationship with me. Nor has he seemingly wanted to. I accepted that. What I find interesting is that he's for the most part extremely placid. In spite of all of his issues. (Unless intoxicated, but that's another story) Whereas my NPD brother has always been anything but placid. I see how he used to assert his "superiority" by telling our NPD mother and/or enabling father anything he found out that painted me in a less than favourable light.

He ended up doing time in jail in his late teens. He was around eighteen years of age at that time. My older brother has done far more time in jail over the years. However, that being said, he at some point actually settled down. And, from what I can see, has somehow managed to be a wonderful father to his two daughters. Who no longer have their biological mother. She died of an asthma attack in her forties. Nonetheless, she was a whole lot of dysfunction herself. And a horrendous trouble maker. At my brother's expense.

Both of those brothers have also done drugs. They are absolutely wrecked because of it. It pains me, yet there's not a thing I can do about it. The one closest in age to me has none of his own teeth left. As for the older one of the two of them: You cannot understand what he's saying when he speaks. It is simply sad beyond any words.

However, none of us have come off unscathed. My sister, who I know I've already mentioned is the "golden child", may not have ever done any drugs or alcohol, but she's had no successful relationship. She's been heavy in debt for I am unsure how long. Perhaps may still be, to an extent. Certainly, becoming carer to both parents was in her interests somewhat financially.

Her and my eldest brother, (who is the most emotionally stable), both mentioned NPD mother and enabling father using a fire poker on them in their childhood years. Did NPD mother and enabling father deny it? You bet. Was that before dementia with our enabling father? Yes. This is the "norm" in such a family dynamic.

My own experiences involved corporal and other forms of punishment. It changed over the years. For the most part, I honestly have no idea what I'd even done to warrant the punishment. All I remember is the actual punishment. No reason. No logic. Simply do as we say, not as we do. In effect.

I recall how elated I felt upon leaving that environment. Interestingly, I did allow NPD mother to manipulate me at that time. Her suggested choice of moving to somewhere about a two hour drive from where they lived, as opposed to further afield, which was what I had been considering was something I took to heart at that time.

Although where I now currently live is only about a three hour drive from there, it's in another direction, and not where anyone seems to want to come to, unless they have to. More or less. Thankfully. Then again, it's always about them. Myself, my wife and daughter should drop everything and come running at their beck and call. Though not any of them would dream of doing anything of that nature on our behalf. Ever. Period.

For me the defining moment was when I had received via text message from my golden child sister a "request" (for want of a better word) to come and look after NPD mother for a few days whilst eldest brother and his wife were away. Oh, and golden child sister was planning a trip to Ireland around that same time (with a friend).

My work was of a casual nature. I would literally have to at my own expense not work for that period, along with the travel and any other costs. I happened to send a text to my eldest brother not long after. Through doing so, I found out through him that no longer was there going to be any trip to Ireland. Also, that I was no longer needed to look after NPD mother. That did it.

There was no gratitude. No appreciation. By this point, I had healed. I actually had mentioned to eldest brother via text could she go into respite care for that time. That's the only reason I found out that anything was any different. My golden child sister hadn't even the regard to let me know of any change. There was therefore no other option than to go no contact with all of them.

My eldest brother shortly thereafter realised that I had changed my mobile phone number. By this point, I had no need to explain anything. To any of them. I now knew my worth. I now knew beyond any doubt that not one of them was deserving of it. And the chances of them ever cognitively realising it were most likely slim to none.

Oh, and for the record, the only reason he found out as soon as he did was because there was an event coming up related to our daughter that I had been keeping him posted about. That's why he contacted my wife, after having failed to have been able to contact me. Otherwise, it might well have been longer.

Okay, so I'm now going to go into quite a bit of detail in relation to the golden child (often narcissistic), NPD parent, scapegoat truth telling child dynamics. Clearly, this is something I relate to on a personal level. It's something I feel is extremely vital for people to truly understand. To get it. The more boxes we tick, the more we will never put ourselves into that kind of dynamic again. It's sufficient to give you even more what you need incentive wise to remain no contact. No matter what. Let the dysfunctional walls fall down all around you. In a sense. It need no longer be something that you have any involvement in.

I want to go into detail about this because I do believe on a subconscious level I knew about my golden child sister's involvement, also how I felt gut wise in regard to her. However, I never saw it as clearly as it actually is: That the NPD parent has groomed the golden child for their role. Also, that they are both working together against the scapegoat "truth teller" child the entire time. I feel many other people like myself may have felt the wrongness, yet it may be somewhat intangible until it's been spelt out beyond a shadow of any doubt.

Don't be fooled. The dynamic between the golden child and the scapegoat child is toxic. To clarify: I am talking about the highly malignant narcissistic "golden child". In some instances, at least one I know of personally, two girls, both adopted by the same couple, have always had a relationship based on unconditional love. This relationship has lasted for several decades. Long after both have left the abusive NPD home environment they were both raised in. And yet, one was most definitely the golden child. The other the scapegoat child. If this is how it is in your own personal instance, you are extremely fortunate. And I am nothing other than happy for that being so in your personal instance.

In fact, it seems that the vast majority of golden children are just "golden": all good, doted on, coddled, and adored. The difference with the narcissistic "golden child" is that they are not so benign. To the extent that they will take the utmost delight in supporting the NPD parent's efforts to destroy the scapegoat child's confidence and self esteem. In my own instance, with just over eighteen years in age between myself and my older golden child sister, this is precisely what has taken place. For many people, the age difference would likely be far less. Therefore, closeness in age may or may not be a factor in this dynamic.

The disordered golden child isn't necessarily the eldest child. Nonetheless, a lot of the time you'll find the oldest child will play out the "golden child/scapegoat dynamic" with the second child within a narcissistic family. What's important to note is that this narcissistic "golden child" will mistreat not solely the scapegoat child, but all of their siblings. All the same, the scapegoated child will endure the most. Why? Because they refuse to go along with the narcissistic golden child's illusions of grandeur. And due to them refusing to accept the belief of the golden child that they're entitled to abuse, steal from others, become aggressive at the slightest criticism, or have complete control over other people.

In essence, the scapegoated child, due to their having honesty and integrity, won't go along with the ruse or charade of "mirroring" or reflecting to the narcissistic golden child as they'd prefer to be mirrored. So, what then results? In effect, with the nod of approval from the narcissistic parent, the malignant golden child smashes the mirror.

I can personally vouch to the truth of this. I've experienced it. My malignant golden child sister gleefully went to my NPD mother without any hesitation with anything and everything related to me. How they relished in twisting whatever they could in regards to me. My malignant golden child sister even began bagging me out to my wife, before it occurred to her that it was my wife. And subsequently stopped. Am I entirely done with both of them? Absolutely. No longer am I available for their toxic waste disposal. Did I mention no contact rocks?

Polarised thinking: that all good or all bad pattern of thinking characterises narcissists. Nope, no shades of grey are able to be seen. It's black. Or it's white. Whilst one person's seen as all good, another person's seen as all bad. At times, there's an alternation of these perceptions in the disordered mind of the narcissist.

This being what it is, the first child may seem all good to the NPD parent. And the second child all bad. Or it may be the other way around. There's no rhyme or reason with a narcissist. And, it may switch. Without warning. Remember, roles in a narcissistic family set up are somewhat fluid. Is it any wonder victims are so drained and depleted?

Without narcissism in the equation, birth order plays a major role in personality development. What this means it that in a healthy family dynamic, the first child is the one most likely to emulate the parents. If the parents are narcissistic, the second child has a problem.

What about the narcissistic golden child? They're often a replica of the NPD parent. They have subconsciously taken on the NPD parent's values, beliefs, and way of life. These beliefs are integrated into all aspects of their life.

This, for me, helped me understand why my NPD mother moved us over ocean to where golden child sister lived at the time (Tasmania) about some forty kilometres out of the nearest town of any real size. Golden child sister's husband was working on mainland Australia, so wasn't around. She had not long had their fourth child when this move took place. Our NPD mother never did that for any other of her offspring. And, to be honest, she did virtually nothing to actually help golden child sister out whilst there, anyway. Still, it must have looked good to others. After all, appearances are everything to a narcissist.

This is where the scapegoat child differs entirely from the NPD parent along with the narcissistic golden child. I am so proud to be able to say this. And so proud that I am the scapegoat child. Here is why: The scapegoated child consciously entirely rejects the NPD parent's beliefs, values, and way of life. Whereas the golden child simply goes along with the NPD parent to get along, the scapegoat child does no such thing. Rather, they consciously question the NPD parent's way of thinking.

Furthermore, the scapegoat child decides to treat people respectfully, disliking how their NPD parent role model treats others. Whilst the golden child models their NPD parent, choosing to treat others based on how their NPD parent role model treats others.

It's not entirely evident as to why the narcissistic golden child takes on the same personality as the NPD parent, nor why the scapegoated child doesn't. It's believed that family dynamics play a part in the creation of both children. However, that being said, the following is clear: the highly malignant golden child isn't nurtured by their NPD parent. Which is precisely why they cannot relay any empathy. Because they have never been shown any empathy.

Empathy is often taught. Meaning that if a child isn't pulled up on their treatment of others and given consequences for it, they do not learn the difference between kindness and unkindness. If a child's not corrected for their behaviour, then they'll think it's fine to behave badly. No one's told them any different. Early on, this child learns that it's okay to do whatever they wish.

How then can it be that the scapegoated child is so different? Is this not a paradox? Consider the good or bad thinking on the part of the NPD parent. It's one way or another. This is why there's a difference, it seems. As a scapegoat child myself, I can attest to what other scapegoat children the world over relate to having been their experience. Which is that we were constantly being pulled up on any poor behaviour. Also, that we were told on an ongoing basis when we weren't treating people properly. As for the golden child, they weren't pulled up. Ever. They were taught that whatever they did was perceived as okay in the NPD parent's eyes, regardless of how vile it may have been. Simply because they were the golden child.

The different, contrasting expectations for the golden and scapegoated child match up with the NPD parent's polarised black or white thinking. The narcissistic golden child was encouraged to take on the selfish, devoid of any empathy behaviour of the NPD parent. The scapegoated child was often told that they were ruthless. Also that they needed to be more empathetic.

Survival on the part of the golden child was related to gaining the NPD parent's approval. More or less. They learnt that to get that approval, they must behave in the judgemental, unempathetic, disgusting way that the NPD parent did. Because if they acted as the scapegoat child: with empathy, concern, and love, they'll be treated as the scapegoat child. Which is basically standing in a corner and having stones thrown at them. Unconsciously, the golden child decided that they might fare better, even gaining some approval, or feigned love and support from the NPD parent if they take on the role of psycho bully. That they'll do better in this messed up family by doing this. No, it's not thought out properly on the part of the golden child. What it boils down to is the mentality of survival of the fittest that some narcissistically inclined children take on.

The extent of malignancy with the golden child basically depends on whether or not they only have one NPD parent to mirror. If so, they're in strife. Big time. However, if there is another parent (codependent) who shows them some love, then they may do better in regards to how malignant they are.

Regarding the scapegoated child: they reject narcissism. They have the empathy gene. They know how to love. Therefore, they can put themselves in another's shoes, as it were, and feel that person's pain. Due to this ability to be able to feel others internal pain, sooner or later it will drive them to speak up about the abuse from the NPD parent. Not only to themself, but also towards the golden child. I know from my own experience, I began to not simply say nothing any longer about my NPD mother. In effect, I started calling her out on her abuse. Speaking up about her ongoing hypocrisy.

Precisely why the scapegoat child is more sensitive to the feelings of others and has more empathy isn't entirely clear. Perhaps it's because they were/are seen as all 'black' (bad) in the mind of the NPD parent. The scapegoated child was/is constantly reminded by the narcissist that they need to be empathetic, kind, and improve upon the innate 'badness' that the narcissist has projected onto them. This treatment by the NPD parent often pushes the scapegoat child to work even harder to prove their goodness to them. This was precisely how I myself used to be.

A lack of entitlement may be the saving grace for the scapegoat child, or; they may simply have been nurtured more than the golden child by the enabling parent (codependent) somewhere along the line. I personally have come to the realisation that any of my good qualities most definitely do come from my enabling father. Certainly not from my NPD mother. However, if he did nurture me more, I genuinely have no recollection of it.

The NPD parent's rejection of the scapegoated child is a double-edged sword. In some ways being rejected pays for this child. How so? Fortunately, they were never embraced with a sick love, nor were any delusions of grandeur thrown their way. I can attest that this is so. They escaped the false self which took over the narcissistic child. Resulting in the silver lining that the damage done to them is somewhat repairable.

The NPD parent's differential treatment of the two

children puts the scapegoat in a position where they begin to see through their golden child sibling. They can see straight through the lie the golden child has fallen victim to. The scapegoated child knows their golden child sibling is not entitled, that they aren't grand, aren't going to be famous, and absolutely not this amazing person the narcissistic parent keeps making out they are. They see how cruel this child is. As a consequence, the scapegoat child openly rejects narcissism. In my own instance, this had to have happened at an extremely young age. It also totally resonates with my own experiences.

What happens when the scapegoat talks about the elephant in the room? The scapegoated child is in big trouble. This NPD mother (father) and son, or NPD mother (father) and daughter duo are the hierarchy. The other child/ren either follows suit, and allows the NPD parent and golden child to control them, without complaining; or they complain, and become scapegoated.

The scapegoated option is the option unintentionally chosen by sometimes the second child, who almost always ends up sparring with the entitled child daily, and complaining endlessly to the NPD parent about the endless abuses incurred from the golden child. Challenging the NPD parent's illusion about their 'special' child ends badly for the scapegoated child. They may spend their entire childhood being pecked at by a psychologically dangerous child, and a psychotic parent.

I feel it vital at this point to add the following: My golden child sister is eighteen years older than me. She is the third child of six. I am the youngest child. She is the second oldest living child. It was the second child who drowned at the age of sixteen. My NPD brother is the fifth child. I wanted to add this so that it's clear that these dynamics are seen to be perhaps somewhat more fluid in a larger NPD parent ruled family.

This golden child represents to the NPD parent everything amazing they see in themselves. The NPD parent lives and breathes through this grandiose, omnipotent, amazing child. This is the child that will defend the narcissist to no end, battle all of the people that continue to harm the NPD parent's ego, and will prove their omnipotence to the people around them. The NPD parent will shine like a star through this child. I know right. Us scapegoats likely have a finger down our throat about now. Because we see through these lies and deceptions.

The scapegoat child strikes blow upon blow to the NPD parent's ego when they point out that the golden child isn't so wonderful after all. That they're flawed, troubled, and mean. This creates a huge narcissistic injury in this parent, who sees everything they love about themselves in this narcissistic child.

The NPD parent doesn't encourage love between the two children. Not that there is any love here. Only pure hatred from the narcissistic golden child towards the scapegoated child. The relationship between these two children is very similar to the account of Cain and Abel as found in the early part of the first bible book of Genesis. The NPD parent deliberately sets this dynamic up for their own vested interests.

This dangerous, toxic dynamic between the two children serves a purpose for the NPD parent, who has deliberately pitted both children against each other. The NPD parent encourages the golden child to try to gain control over the scapegoat child. The NPD parent never intends to encourage love and harmony. Rather, they allow the golden child to abuse the scapegoat, and they don't bat an eyelid. It's a hate fest, where this dynamic duo attack, and discredit the scapegoated child any chance they get.

The NPD parent will share the children's secrets with each child, paint each child as black behind each other's backs, and will feign victimhood when the situation explodes, and the children blow up at one another. This friction between the children is just another way of gaining attention from anyone who will listen when the NPD parent explains to people how they have these two terrible children who can't get along. Of course, as always, the NPD parent will do anything for fuel, and drama. Even if it means triangulating their children.

The golden child at this stage is a fully fledged narcissist. They operate with a false self, and they totally believe in the illusion – that they truly are grandiose, a hero, and omnipotent. When the scapegoated child challenges the narcissistic illusion, they are pummelled, turned against, lied about, and smashed down by the narcissistic child to the NPD parent, who just goes along with it. I've personally experienced all of this.

The situation by this stage is too far gone, and the relatively good-natured enabling parent can't get the situation between the two children under control because the narcissist isn't on the same page as them.

How does the narcissistic golden child treat their siblings? The narcissistic golden child doesn't love any of their siblings and treats each of them terribly. They will, however, feign kindness towards the sibling or siblings', that they feel are easier to control, and are more compliant appliances; especially if it serves them in some way.

The golden child will use these children as pawns to antagonize the scapegoated child. They will share something with a more compliant child and reject the scapegoat when they ask if they too can have some of whatever it is being shared. They will allow the more compliant child to engage with, or play with them while informing the scapegoat that they are not invited to play. As time goes on, and the scapegoat becomes more difficult to control, the golden child will even try to brainwash the other siblings into believing that the scapegoated child is fundamentally flawed, and that everybody must exclude them in some way or another.

This behaviour worsens in adulthood, and often results in family mobbing. The golden child and NPD parent are always the ringleaders in family mobbing against the scapegoat. The golden child will rage at their siblings, laugh at them in a condescending manner; use them when they please, and reject them if they suddenly need help, support, or empathy.

However, this being said, the more compliant sibling, or siblings, will not endure the harassment that the scapegoated child endures; unless of course, they question the golden child's control. If one child is already the scapegoat, the golden child has no need to go after the other siblings'. They already have a punching bag.

The golden child will provoke, and provoke and provoke the scapegoat child into arguments, while never antagonizing the more compliant siblings in such a way. They will pick this child to bits. They will pick at their entire being. When they become upset and react to the abuse, they will be told that they are unhinged, unstable and crazy.

There are two sets of rules for the golden child and the scapegoat child. If this child rages and screams at everyone, the NPD parent doesn't move on in to protect the children from the abuse. Instead, they accept it as the norm. However, if the scapegoat loses it because they can't tolerate the golden child's abuse anymore, they will never hear the end of it from the NPD parent. They will be told they are neurotic, highly strung, and a bad person; whereas the golden child's faults will be swept underneath the carpet as though they never happened. They are all good, and the scapegoat is all bad. The narcissistic golden child is groomed to be the NPD parent's soldier. This NPD parent doesn't like anybody. Nobody will ever be good enough, and everybody who comes into contact with them is a potential scapegoat.

The NPD parent literally grooms the golden child into becoming their soldier. The golden child (who will do anything to be accepted in this rejecting narcissistic family system) falls victim to the NPD parent's manipulations, and believes in the NPD parent's lies told continually about potential scapegoats. The golden child is the ultimate 'bark dog'. This child behaves as though they are at war with everyone.

The NPD parent lives through the golden child. They encourage the golden child to trash talk everybody that comes into the room, be on the lookout for potential scapegoats, and to judge people harshly, with no room for error. Other people's faults become the golden child's focus, instead of their own. Judge judge judge.

Often this duo will be a mother and a son, a mother and her daughter, a father, and daughter, or father and son. They are best friends and will conquer the world together. If anyone challenges the system, the golden child is there with the NPD parent to organize the smear campaign. Sadly, the object of the smear campaign is often the family scapegoat.

Why does the golden child have it in for the scapegoat

with such intensity? This is about the golden child's sense of entitlement. The NPD parent felt entitled enough to create a mini me and taught the child early on that they are entitled to exercise complete control over the scapegoat child, and everybody else they come into contact with.

This kind of golden child becomes that narcissistic adult in the room that a lot of us have probably met – the one who must have complete control over the actions, words, thoughts, and beliefs of everybody within their environment. The scapegoat is just meant to sit down and shut up. The malignant golden child's sense of entitlement will not allow this child to accept that other people have human rights to a different opinion or different ideas from them.

Pulling the golden child up on their behavior, or disagreeing with their opinion on any given topic is seen by the golden child as severely manipulative behaviour by the perpetrator of such an offense (usually the scapegoat). Even though all their behaviour is severely manipulative. A hypocrite like the NPD parent.

The NPD parent is completely to blame for this over exaggerated sense of grandiosity and entitlement in the golden child because this parent taught the golden child that they have complete control over everybody in their environment. The first victim under the complete control of the golden child was the scapegoat. The NPD parent gave the golden child this position of power over the scapegoat and set the golden child up to believe that they will have control over anybody in their space.

What happens to the scapegoat's relationship with the golden child in adulthood? The relationship between the scapegoat and the golden child is often so damaged that the scapegoat outwardly resents the golden child. They don't have a problem challenging the golden child's false self. They don't like them, and they aren't going to hide it, regardless of the repercussions.

This person damaged the scapegoat so badly in childhood that there is no way that the scapegoated child will mirror back to the golden child that they are grand and omnipotent. The scapegoat can't be controlled. The scapegoat is a continued reminder to the golden child that they are truly an abuser and a dangerous person.

So what does the golden child do? They smash the mirror over and over, with the help of the NPD parent, until the scapegoat eventually walks out of the family.

Eventually, many narcissistic golden children ruin the scapegoat's reputation in adult life and turn their siblings against them, as well as the enabling parent. Rigid, weak enabling family members often just go with it. The scapegoat is often so terribly shamed and humiliated by these people that they are advised by their therapist to leave the entire family.

Does anyone support the scapegoat? It's unlikely. There appears to be an inability for the scapegoats' siblings, even the less narcissistically inclined siblings to empathise with the intensity of the scapegoat's pain; because if they could empathise at all, they would stand up for their sibling, and actually ask their golden child sibling, or the NPD parent, to stop abusing the scapegoat. However, most of the NPD parent's children turn a blind eye, look the other way, and allow for the scapegoated child to get pecked and pecked and pecked, until there is literally no soul left to peck at. It often becomes a case of 'well thank goodness it isn't me.'

The narcissistic golden child convinces the other siblings who fail to support their scapegoated sibling that the scapegoat is unhinged, mentally ill, and needs help with emotional regulation. The golden child also says these vile things about the scapegoat in the hope of escaping all accountability. It works. Oh does it work.

Scapegoated individuals are strong, often creative, and intelligent. They are often the most empathetic child in the narcissistic family, which is the primary reason why they are so targeted. When they leave the narcissistic family they take these traits with them, grieve the family, heal, and begin traveling the road less traveled by family members in the narcissistic family; the road to recovery. The scapegoat has integrity. They never back down on this integrity, and they usually go on to have very fulfilling lives. The narcissistic family members either stay united in chaos or turn on each other.

I've been down this precise path. I know what it's like as the scapegoated child. I know that I'm in the best place in my entire life since walking away from my own narcissistic family members. Truly, if you are in the same shoes, congratulations. Better days are ahead. Simply better and better. Don't be hard on yourself. You're a beautiful soul. You deserve better. You always have.

9

WHAT KEPT YOU VICTIMISED
&
HOW TO CHANGE IT

By now, my dear friend, you might be thinking you know a lot about narcissism, particularly narcissistic abuse. And compared to what you knew previously, you likely do know far more. However, self love recovery is a journey. The underlying reason you likely have suffered this abuse is because of your beautiful nature. You are a caring, kind, empathetic individual. Unfortunately, who cared too much for the wrong person.

Despite what you may now know, the narcissist/s in your life could only control and manipulate you, and keep you coming back for more abuse for one reason: You had wounds that hadn't been addressed. Which they honed in on. And targeted.

That underlying lack of self love is the root cause of why you were victimised for as long as you were. I know it isn't easy to face up to that. To say to yourself: It wasn't solely the narcissist/s in my life's fault. It was partly mine, too. Hey, I had to acknowledge that myself. It's the only way that we are able to move forward.

Bottom line is this: That victim versus persecutor dialogue running inside of you needs to be in the past. Past tense. You are strong. You are a survivor. You are a warrior even. Otherwise, that sort of mentality is going to keep you trapped. It's going to keep you stuck. And you won't have learnt enough to go inwards to change. Meaning you'll be little to no different than before. And it's highly probable that you'll still attract narcissists.

There are no boundaries with a narcissist. Therefore, the only way to change attracting them is for you to change. For you to do the inner work. For you to finally heal, get healthy self esteem and self worth. And you totally can do just that.

In effect, you have been addicted to self love deficit disorder. This is the problem that's kept you in victim mode. The core challenge for people who are codependent. Despite the fact that everything in the relationship with the narcissist/s in your life was what you gave, you still stayed. Despite not getting it reciprocated. Now you know why.

If you had self love, you wouldn't have stood for the pain and horror from these relationships. Would you, my dear friend? It's okay to be honest here. It's okay to let this hit you. And yes, it will hit you hard. That's as it should be. We have to feel this, to allow ourselves to feel it. Or nothing can change. I know that this hit me like a freight train.

Therefore, this means codependency is actually a trauma disorder. Trauma attachment, like explained in great detail earlier in this book: i.e. Stockholm Syndrome. The solution is self love.

In order to change that lack of self love, you need to eliminate the underlying core shame and pathological loneliness. That's the addiction. You were addicted to it. Like a drug. At the root of this is that you were raised by at least one parent who was a pathological narcissist. If another parent was around, that other parent was codependent: self love deficit disordered.

Being raised in an environment by an NPD parent and a codependent parent who couldn't necessarily protect you, ensured that you experienced attachment trauma. In other words, you weren't able to feel either loved, safe, protected, or respected. Resulting in physical, emotional and psychological trauma during your formative years. The end result? Core shame. Attachment trauma is unconscious. Whereas core shame is semi conscious. Codependents are conscious of feeling bad about who they are. Core shame is a distorted definition of self where you feel only as good as what you do. Stemming from core shame comes the all pervasive feeling of pathological loneliness.

This feeling can only be medicated or felt to go away (albeit temporarily) when in a relationship. So long as a person stays in this state, unconsciously they will be attracted to pathological narcissists. It's a recipe for disaster. Over and over again. The narcissist convinces you to help them in a way that ends up hurting you. You've been addicted to the drug they've been selfishly providing you with.

Self love is the only thing, the only solution to neutralise the person who is self love deficient. It's also the only thing to neutralise any attraction to pathological narcissists ever again. It's a process. However, it will permanently change you, along with your life for the better. It can even free you from depression. The ultimate goal for you is what's termed as self love abundance.

And please don't worry that it's anything other than healthy self esteem and healthy self worth. Because, my dear friend, that's basically what it is. Not the egotistical kind. Knowing your worth. Valuing that. And when you do, you'll be amazed at how differently your life is. How much smoother and better it is. No longer will anyone be able to drain you as previously had happened. No longer will you attract narcissists. It's similar to as if you have a can of "narcissist be gone". Which reminds me: In the interim, if you remember that everything coming out of the narcissist/s in your life's mouth is lies, that will help keep you from being supply for them.

An excellent outline of the stages in recovering from self love deficit disorder to self love abundance is as follows (as outlined by Ross Rosenberg): The Ten Stage Self-Love Recovery Model: Getting to Self-Love Recovery:

1) Hitting bottom: Introducing hope
2) Understanding the Human Magnet Syndrome i.e. Relational chemistry
3) Understanding Self Love Deficit Disorder Addiction and Pathological Loneliness
4) Preparing for the Narcissistic Storm (Mastering Power & Control Dynamics)
5) Setting Boundaries in a Hostile Environment
6) Maintaining Safe and Secure Boundaries
7) Resolving/Integrating Unconscious Trauma (Healing Attachment Trauma)
8) Transitioning from Self Love Deficit Disorder to Self Love Abundance
9) Practicing and Enjoying Self Love Driven Relationships
10) Achieving Self Love Abundance or Self Love Recovery

A huge thing in healing your attachment trauma is acknowledging and accepting that it was never your fault that your parents (either codependent OR NPD) simply didn't know how to love unconditionally. They didn't even love themselves. Hurt people hurt others. Wounded people wound others. They were so caught up in themselves, in each other, in dodging the bullets (codependent enabling parent in relation to the NPD parent) they couldn't love you how you deserved to be loved.

Once the narcissist loses that emotional connection hold they've had over you due to being self love deficient, you no longer engage with them. The sooner that's dissolved, the better. Giving up the delusion, the fantasy that they'll ever change dissolves that. They are simply incapable of such change. You, on the other hand, are extremely capable of it.

Address your mother wound. Address your father wound. Tend lovingly to these wounds. Your brain is likely still in a state of fight or flight from your childhood. Complex PTSD or PTSD can cause the following in you:

You can't concentrate. You can't sleep. You feel angry that you have been put in this position. You feel worthless. You feel like you always have to be vigilant, ready to take on another attack. You can't seem to handle the simplest task. You feel like a doormat most of the time. You feel depressed most of the time. You feel like you want to be alone most of the time. You may sometimes wish you were dead. You feel like you are in pain most of the time. You feel spacey like you can't think straight. You have constant nightmares.

A lot of this can stem from trauma attachment. Having parents who simply didn't know how to love themselves. There's different forms of treatments available. If you wish to, feel free to research these. If you don't feel comfortable about a certain treatment, don't allow yourself to feel pressured to accept if (if offered), or as if it is your only option. Quite simply, it isn't. However, getting rid of the toxic guilt and shame that the NPD parent projected onto you is a massive relief and weight gone. I know because I had it projected onto me.

The narcissist/s in your life have never cared about you, will never care about you, and will only ever treat you as an extension of themselves. Make no mistake about that. Don't allow it any longer. Only you can do the inner work. Only you.

The best thing you can do is heal so that you can thrive. To be that loving parent to yourself that you didn't have. Once you stop trying to fix other people, watch what happens. Narcissists control so that they aren't controlled. But, it's weakness, my dear friend. Not strength. Unconsciously, you may have also tried to control others. Let this go. All of it. Go more into your heart, and not so much in your head. Get the criticism and judgement out of your internal dialogue. That was programming from your earliest years that you had no control over. Reprogram it.

Practice self care. Initiate positive self talk. As a rule of thumb for yourself: If you wouldn't say it to a friend, don't say it to yourself. If you don't want to do something for someone, don't do it. Manipulative people (NPD or others) will continue to trample all over you and boundaries until you raise the bar. Until you establish boundaries. Until you stop feeling as if you have to explain anything to anyone. You'll be amazed how different things are when you institute these changes.

Self care is something you've likely rarely, if ever done. Because you were too busy doing for other people. It's basically activities that replenish you. Things that you like doing. If you can have one day a week for you, to do what you enjoy, it makes a massive difference. If a day a week is out of the equation, be sure that you still regularly do things that you enjoy. Believe me, the world will still turn.

Here's some self care tips: Anything related to nature is excellent. It might be a walk outside. Practicing deep breathing. (This can also be good to manage anxiety) These activities needn't cost anything in a monetary way. And that's as it should be: the best things in life are free. A trip to your local library. Reading a favourite book. Or a book about something that interests you. Spending time with a pet. (Pets can be extremely therapeutic, and many animals will shower you with unconditional love) Cook a nice meal. Colouring or doodling. Listen to your favourite music. Listen to calming music even. Playing solitaire with real cards. Call a friend who listens without judgement. Meet a friend for lunch or dinner. Or maybe even for just a coffee. Sit somewhere in a public area and simply watch people.

The following quote is something to keep in mind from here on, my dear friend. Please make this your personal goal: "When you know better you do better. You love yourself better and make decisions that protect you from harm. Make progress not regress. Stay moving forward. No reason to look back."

Once we see in ourselves a lot more than we had, we can see the same in others. This changes us for the better. We simply cannot go back. On the flipside of that, we can't see in others what we don't see in ourselves. We can't recognise it in others if we can't recognise it in ourselves. Isn't that what kept us in this unconscious, painful "dance" with the narcissist/s in our lives in the first place?

I look forward to knowing you will be doing what's best for you and your emotional and mental wellbeing from this point on, my dear friend. We paid a price dearly for not knowing how to do this in our past. Now, we've learned the lessons, we can do better, because we know better. You know all those chances you'd dished out to the narcissist/s in your life? Which, of course, were to no avail. Well, how about giving yourself those chances instead? How about giving yourself the brand new start you've always deserved? How about doing that? Is that a deal? Well, is it?

10

HOW TO PREVENT NARCISSISTIC ABUSE & BE THE BEST YOU CAN BE – FOR LIFE

For me, the decision to go no contact with biological family members came over time. I went grey rock with my NPD mother during one year. In which, I, along with my wife and daughter, were manipulated into going to visit/babysit her. At our own expense, of course.

On our way back from a long trip, (requiring an overnight stay), I sent NPD mother a text message about where we were staying overnight. (We had to go through the place where she lived the following day between where we were staying and where we lived) What happened the following day as we were leaving the place where NPD mother lived? My mobile phone rang. It was her. We were actually eating lunch at Hungry Jacks, on the outskirts of the place where NPD mother lives. I didn't answer it. I let it go to voicemail. I'd learned my lesson. I didn't contact her again of any of my own initiative. When I later listened to the voicemail, it was quite funny. NPD mother basically was after some supply from me, trying to control us, wanting to know where we were. I never responded after that. I got three text messages after the following couple of months related to three people we knew in common having passed. Yes, NPD people love misery and sadness. That's why you always hear bad news like that from them. Besides, it's a chance to get some supply and attention.

How can they pass on that?

So, it comes to the date of my birth. I turned forty two on this day. I get a text message (after supply) from NPD mother. How was I, blah, blah, blah. (Like I'd fall for her "caring" charade) I smiled as I thought of my reply. I'd healed. I was genuinely in the best place of my life. And I texted as much by way of reply, knowing she was not going to like this at all. Guess what? There was no reply and no further messages from her in the following three months whatsoever. And then I changed my mobile phone number, and only gave it to those people I wanted to have it. No biological family members were given it.

We give people who do nothing for us far too many chances. Enough is enough. They say once the scapegoat child goes no contact, the rest of the family basically turn on each other. I don't know. And I don't care. Why should I? I'd been emotionally parentified for so long. It was never me who should have fulfilled their emotional needs. I was robbed of a childhood. I had to be responsible. I had to be an adult, whilst a child, in effect.

And all they did was continue to abuse. As someone who read my first autobiographical account of my childhood years, "Surviving Childhood", (available on Payhip.com) said to me, "Your parents were nasty." Pure and simple. That's it in essence. My NPD brother and golden child sister too. Oh, they'll try and use the blackmail card. Don't fall for it. Once you are an adult, if you aren't treated as an adult, then you aren't the problem. Remember that.

And as your emotional intelligence increases, you'll find your life truly can be beautiful. Every day. Enjoy it. Drink it in. For so long, like myself, it was all about others. No more.

Look after your own peace of mind. Your own emotional wellbeing. Your own mental health. If that requires cutting people out of your life, then so be it. Because, you know what? You'll be just fine.

The control they hold over you is thinking you won't be okay. But, in reality, they don't want you to find out that you will. That's why they have no boundaries. You're seen as that shiny toy they can do what they want with. And when to them, that toy's shine is gone, they'll be done with it. Then pick it up again. If it's still around and contactable. So don't be.

So, a little now related to being a codependent empath. Because, the fact that you have been victimised by a narcissist/s means that that is what you are. (In case you didn't already know) The scapegoat child is an empath. Stuck in empath codependency mode only, you'll likely have black and white thinking. You'll see yourself as the victim, and everyone else as a persecutor. Emotional intelligence changes that.

Here's what is going on when you are in trouble with a narcissist. As in your downward spiral with the narcissist/s in your life. You have a hyperactivated attachment system. Meaning you'll feel intense closeness, intense chemistry, even an intense fascination with the narcissist at the outset of the relationship. At this point, this will override your cognitive faculties. Because it is, after all, a hyperactivated attachment system. Despite that underneath, you'll likely realise that you knew all along that it was too good to be true. That there was too much flattery. However, that internal knowing wasn't fully used. The "feel good" type chemicals have overrided your cognitive faculties.

This is accompanied by the need to please. You want to

be agreeable. The fear of upsetting the narcissist. Concern as to how you are coming across to them. A lot of monitoring yourself. Which leads to the inner critic and judge in you being triggered. That strong internal critic. Basically, the narcissist pushes the codependent empath's buttons. Hence, the toxic "attraction". Can you see why it's been addictive?

That codependent empath need to please puts you on a high alert mode to the needs of the narcissist. For example, the excessive giving on your part to the narcissist. To your detriment. However, to the narcissist's advantage. They'll use this to trigger guilt, to gaslight, to make you doubt your reality. That inner critic is at this point maximally focused on yourself, rather than the narcissist.

So, the narcissist is putting the focus on you as the codependent empath. Their comments, suggestions, and so on. Because of these three things being all on: the hyperactivated attachment system, the need to please, and the strong internal critic, you lose any grounded authority. Thus, rendering you vulnerable to the narcissist. However, this is also unsustainable.

Which is why you hit that brick wall. And when you do, you begin to see the dark side of those same three things. And so they become distorted. Leading you to feel resentment, cynicism, and hostility. So, you are then aware of how your attachment system has been hijacked, how you were lied to, and how you consistently denied your own needs.

Now, that inner critic that had been directed inward: to yourself, becomes directed at other parties. Not solely the narcissist. Also other people who are in your life. Meaning you become extremely critical and judgemental of others as that strong inner critic is aimed outwardly. Resulting in the destroying of relationships, creating deep rifts, even with your support base. That need to please now flips. So, instead of being highly agreeable, you become highly disagreeable.

Therefore, you, as a codependent empath can actually become quite tyrannical to those you consider lower in the dominance hierarchy. And you may act with high levels of displaced aggression towards others. Perhaps seeking retribution and becoming highly resentful. Not solely towards the narcissist. But also to others in your life. Why? Because you feel these people have let you down.

The hyperactivated attachment system isn't sustainable. That's why you in codependent empath mode get quickly burnt out. Causing you to have your attachment system shut down. And to have great difficulty in any sort of closeness to others. A mistake you likely make at this point is to surround yourself with people who confirm your distorted view of the world. Alienating people who could give you a reality check.

Therefore, you, at this point, view people as against you who aren't. Those in your support base and network. You are becoming highly isolated, along with highly resentful and cynical. This is that victim versus persecutor type thinking referred to earlier. All of this helped me understand my former unhealed codependent empath self in an entirely new light. I hope it has for you as well.

Those wounds from your earliest time in life can no longer be used against you once you are in an ongoing state of self love abundance. You also view people in a different light to previously. This is because your emotional intelligence is far sharper than previously. You connect on a deeper level with people, yet they still have boundaries, and so do you. It's a much healthier, happier, thriving state. Also far more balanced.

You see red flags. You no longer are "needy" of others. Your relationships in general improve. That aching loneliness that used to be inside of you no longer exists. You do what you enjoy. Without any guilt. Without any shame. And yet, you are still a kind, empathetic person in your nature. A far more confident one. With self esteem. With self worth.

Don't forget that feelings are telling us something. That's why we suffered for so long, too. We had our feelings invalidated constantly. It became the norm. It thus became unsafe to feel. We had to numb feelings. Push them down. Stuff them down even. Which, in my instance, and perhaps yours too, resulted in depression.

So, the difference comes when we tune into our feelings. When we feel anxiety, what is it that our body is trying to tell us? "I don't like it. I don't like this. I can't handle this." Let your body know that you have heard what it's telling you. This might sound silly, but, it works.

I'll give you a personal example. I sometimes get anxious with traffic. Now, obviously, traffic is something we have no control over. What I will do is say to myself whilst feeling the anxiety something like this: "Thank you, body. I appreciate you letting me know that you don't like this. I don't know of anyone who likes traffic. It's out of our control, isn't it? But, it's okay. We're doing great. We are safe. We just need to adjust accordingly to the traffic. Thank you for letting me know."

Guess what? It works. The feeling dissipates. I feel calmer. Try it. When we feel something, it's information our body is giving us. We simply need to tune in more. That gut feeling about someone. Goodness knows we have had plenty of those. It's likely our body letting us know that our boundaries aren't being respected. It even feels invasive, doesn't it?

That pushing feelings down was a coping mechanism in our childhood. It simply was unsafe to express ourselves. If it wasn't an explosive reaction from our parents, it was the ongoing communication from them and our siblings that they couldn't care less about us. Or our feelings. We did our best to survive in a hostile environment. If we hadn't done that, who knows how much worse things would have been?

We lost touch with our inner self. And all their negativity was soaked up like a sponge into our little minds. We weren't stupid. We were anything but. We did what we had to do. However, as an adult, it no longer serves us well. I speak from too many years experience in this regard.

So, what are some lifestyle changes you need to make? One is to be in bed by half past ten at night. You might have previously been a night owl, burning the candle at both ends, then waking up as if you have been hit by a bus. You may have used a lot of stimulants to get through the day. And have been plagued by sleep problems.

A wind down ritual in the evening is suggested. Turning off of technology and dimming lights at least one hour prior to going to bed is optimal. It's crucial that you also have a time that you wake up at. A time that is consistent. Self regulating your body clock is what you are doing by doing this. Highly beneficial.

Another thing you should do is to have a breakfast that's rich in protein. Without spelling it out for you, you are basically after consuming food that isn't broken down quickly. Nor carbohydrate rich. That kind of "food" will (if it hasn't been already) wreak havoc with your fight or flight system. And your blood sugar will be all over the place. You think you need that, on top of everything else you've been dealing with?

Now, it's time to moderate your coffee consumption. Empaths have a lot of coffee. Up to eight cups a day. I myself love coffee, but there's not a chance I have that many cups a day. Drinking excessive amounts of coffee puts us in that fight or flight mode. Creating adrenal fatigue. It's also going to dehydrate you. Meaning you should be sure to consume plenty of water during the day. It's well known that having the bulk of water consumed in the earlier part of the day is best.

Which is the next thing you should do. Keep hydrated. Throughout the day. Water often makes any minor headache (caused by dehydration) or tiredness dissipate. In other words, water can give you an energy lift. Sipping is the best way to consume water, as opposed to having large amounts at a time. Therefore, be sure you have a water bottle or container on hand during the day. With water in it.

Depletion of magnesium is also something you want to avoid. Heart palpitations, migraines, tension headaches, anxiety, insomnia, muscle twitches and cramps are all indications that you require more magnesium. Increase magnesium rich foods in your diet. Along with a magnesium supplement that you take regularly.

You've got to start looking after yourself. And if you are truly honest with yourself, you know that it's likely you haven't. Until now. Thriving, the ongoing goal that you now are working towards involves doing what's good for you. Not anything that's to your detriment.

Your inner dialogue from this point on now should go along these lines:

Can I do what this person has asked of me to do and honour myself also?

How do I really feel about what they have asked of me?

Do I really want to do what they've asked, or am I simply seeking to try and gain their approval, to please them, albeit at my own expense?

What does my gut instinct indicate?

Is this person used to me saying yes, and simply taking advantage of me?

Is this person manipulating and/or abusing me?

Does this person ever reciprocate by doing anything for me?

Or is the relationship with this person actually all one way on my part?

What's the loving adult self way to respond to this situation/request/demand?

As opposed to the wounded child thing that I've done for so long?

Has this person ever actually done anything for me for any reason other than for a truly altruistic motive?

Or does there always have to be an egoic payoff in it for them?

How many other things/commitments do I have to do?

Is this a win win situation?

Is this person simply playing the victim/martyr?

If I agree, where will that agreement end up leading me to?

You get the idea. This is part of what you need to do to cease people pleasing, my dear friend.

Once you are complete in your enoughness, this will no longer be an issue. But, hey, it never hurts to have more to help you. It's going to be new for you. As it was for me.

Now, it's time to have a look at some of the destructive fantasies you're bound to have after the narcissist has left. Even though this is actually the best thing for you. That being said, these no longer affect you when you have accepted the painful realities about the narcissist/s in your life. I have to be honest, in my codependent empath state, I totally had these too.

11

UNDERSTANDING THE FIVE DESTRUCTIVE FANTASIES THAT HELPED YOU SURVIVE NARCISSISTIC ABUSE SO YOU CAN THRIVE

As a brief aside before going into the five destructive fantasies that empaths have, it needs to be understood that these are a way to lessen the emotional pain that the empath is feeling. I know from personal experience that this is truly horrendous, so anything that would reduce it feels worthy to cling to. Unfortunately, these are fantasies. And they do have a destructive effect on us. They literally keep us trapped. Locked up in the negative narcissistic cycle of abuse. Even after the narcissist has left. They also end up causing us more emotional pain when we cling to them. Until we see past them to reality.

The first of the destructive fantasies that empaths have after the narcissist has left is that the narcissist/s will admit their mistakes and acknowledge the pain that they have caused you.

Why is this a fantasy? Because if it were true, the person in question would not be a narcissist. If the narcissist could admit their mistakes and acknowledge the pain that they have caused, then by definition they would not be a narcissist.

Another destructive fantasy is that after they have left, your suffering will break through to the narcissist, and will make them realise what they have done to you. Why is this a fantasy?

Because one of the main elements of narcissism is a lack of empathy. If it could be a reality, then this person is not a narcissist.

These beliefs could be termed as unrealistic. As a type of magical thinking. Oh if only they could be true. But, they cannot. Accepting that is in your best interests.

Another destructive fantasy that the empath has after the narcissist has left is that you'll be able to see evidence of the narcissist suffering because of what they have done to you. For example, that you will see evidence of them suffering because someone has done the same to them. Or that you will get to witness them suffer some catastrophe in their life. For instance, that you'll see their business fail. Or get to see some divine retribution fall upon them. And that you will be witness or privy to this. However, narcissists are shameless. Yes, shameless. A core feature of narcissism is that they have a defence against feeling shame, therefore they're shameless. They therefore refuse to suffer. They refuse to let life teach them lessons.

Because there's this ongoing need to maintain the grandiosity. The entitlement. Even if the narcissist was actually suffering in their life, they would refuse to show it to you. They would have to keep up the veneer. Also, they would very swiftly find a way through their various defense mechanisms to ensure that that level of suffering wouldn't reach the conscious level. They would project it away, devalue the source of the suffering, because there's a failure to learn, a failure of wisdom, a lack of any growth in the narcissist.

This is an error in the empath's thinking: assuming that they'll be privy to this in the narcissist's life. That there'll be concrete evidence of it. It's nothing other than a destructive fantasy, my dear friend. That keeps a person locked into the narcissist's orbit. And into the emotional pain.

Another destructive fantasy the empath has after the narcissist has left is that they will be able to prove their superiority to the narcissist, and show them that they have lost out. By leaving, or by being abusive, that they've lost something really good. However, the narcissist defends against feelings of loss or envy by devaluing the other person. It's in reality an impossibility. They'd have to suffer a catastrophic psychological regression. Something they're not going to very easily do.

The final destructive fantasy the empath has after the narcissist has left is that everyone else in the narcissist's life will see them as you do or have done. That they'll be exposed to the world. That they'll be lonely and depressed. That their business partner, their parents, their next partner is going to see the truth about them that you know. Highly unrealistic. Narcissists are expert chameleons.

There can be neither validation, empathy or genuine remorse from a narcissist. It's all fake. It's fake empathy. Fake love. Fake apologies. True apologies equates with someone genuinely trying better. And with changed behaviour. Not out of any kind of payoff for their ego either.

The most I ever got out of my NPD mother was (as she haughtily looked down her nose) "We weren't perfect parents". No kidding. The understatement of the millennium. However, there it was: her having to assert her "superiority" like a pigeon strutting around pooping wherever it goes. On whatever. On whoever.

I'd held onto the delusional fantasy for decades that one day she was going to change, one day she was going to make up for all that she had done. Talk about hopelessly optimistic. Now, what I wait for is for her to pass. I gave my heart, soul, my everything for literally nothing. It was never my "job" to fill the emotional needs of a dysfunctional nightmare of a family.

That unconsciousness of our wounds is what keeps us trapped. I wish I'd woken up sooner. Yes, I do. It took me turning forty to begin unravelling it all. But, our healing journey is at a different rate to everyone else's. And that's okay. I've not remained stuck, by any means. I have such a wonderful peace now, each and every single day. That I'd not trade for anything.

To know that I know my true worth now. Finally. To know that I am enough. To know that I can pick and choose what I accept or don't accept, and not care either way what people think. Take it or leave it. I have nothing to prove. To anyone. I have nothing to say in my "defense" anymore. I choose to simply be.

Not that that means I am a pushover. By no means. Far from it. I don't "cower" anymore. If I have to speak up, I'll speak up. However, I simply choose what I spend my energy on. If I sense it isn't worth wasting my breath on someone, I won't. It's a newfound wisdom. From what I've learned. Seeing so much more in others now, as well as myself has given me that. It will give you that, too, my dear friend.

I want you to know that you did what you thought you had to to survive in a relationship with the narcissist/s in your life. I know I did. As I got older, I started voicing disagreement with my NPD mother. I was also the only one who warned my then future sister in law about my

NPD brother. She wished she'd listened to me. She told my NPD mother and golden child sister this, amongst others. He'd never revealed to her that he was an alcoholic. Imagine that. I didn't know then what I knew now, but I sure did know what a waste of space he was. And still is. What I said, (it was on social media) was: "Are you sure about this?" I was trying to warn her. Interestingly, the day that he selected to marry her in Hong Kong, in a registry office, (how romantic) was, of course, the date of my birth. I find it rather humourous now, considering that it was never a real marriage on his part. If he'd hoped to rain on my parade, well, it didn't work.

Oh, and never marry someone you have only known through social media and/or over the phone. It's tough enough in person. Talk about a handicap. Works for the narcissist, though. Just fine and dandy. They can be on their best behaviour without the mask falling, the true self reveal.

They are not going to learn anything. How can they? When they refuse to. Any kind of self reflection, any kind of humility, any kind of anything remotely even like that is what they constantly defend against. Their defense mechanisms are all related to that. I don't know about you, but when you wake up to this as reality, how can you continue with them as previously?

What I say can be taken however someone wishes to take it: You simply cannot have any kind of relationship with an emotional toddler. Well, not of any substance. If you have no problem with that, then, by all means, prove the countless number of people who have also been abused by a narcissist wrong.

There is no emotional regulation. They're like a wild animal. If they have no concept of what they are doing as being wrong, then how is it that when they wish to, they can put on their best, sanest false self for the benefit of others, and make you appear crazy?

I have to laugh when I reflect to a time when my NPD brother visited us. Now, this is someone who at this point in his life had no long term relationship happening. He'd also long since had the two women who had had three children to him between them go no contact. He had not seen any of those children. Both women had enough self worth to not allow it. They did what they had to do so that he couldn't. Anyway, I digress.

So, he's visiting, and makes some remark to me about parenting in regards to my daughter. Hilarious. As always, the hypocrite. There's no way any of his children would've gotten anything from him in the way of what's referred to here in Australia as maintenance payments. I know for sure that both women who had had children to him would've simply cut their losses and ran. Without hesitation. Knowing that there would never be any accountability or responsibility on his part. Yet, I know definitely that they moved on with their lives. At least one of them found a good man who she married. And had several children with. The other one raised the two children herself.

He never sought out contact with them. He never would have cared to see them. Ever. Yes, that was in their best interests. It doesn't matter what you do for a narcissist, it's never going to be enough. And they'll expect more. Do you still want to put your hand up for that, my dear friend?

When my golden child sister inflicted NPD mother on us to have here for a few days whilst she went away, there was no appreciation expressed for it. Not one of them cared if it was at our expense. Also, that I had just gotten out of work. But, sure, dump her here. Sure, I'll drive her back a three hour drive, then drive back here myself. There is never anything but them that matters. Truly.

And she tried to get supply from me, bemoaning how she felt safer at either the home where golden child sister lived with her as her carer at, or my eldest brother and his wife's home. Poor diddums. And I know why. Because, I wasn't interested in investing as much by this time. I was beginning to wake up to reality. I consciously spent as little time with her as possible. This was at the end of the year where I'd written that revealing childhood autobiography. As if we wanted her with us in the first place. It was just drama, drama, drama. Even the music I was playing in the car on the trip taking her home. Nope. She couldn't like that, could she? Whatever she could look down her nose at, she would. Her taste in music has always been "vastly superior". In her deluded view.

The one thing that she did like was that I'd been able to buy a somewhat better car about a year previous. And that she was able to travel in it. That was about it. And that was clearly about it reflecting well on her. I tell you: these people are truly something else.

Now, what are you going to do from here on, my dear friend? Heal your unconscious wounds? Yes. Love your inner child? Yes. Be the parent to that inner child that it never had? Yes. Turn all of that empathy, love, compassion and more inwards to yourself? Yes. Get rid of programming that is dysfunctional, and that you had no control over? That has had a far reaching effect on you and handicapped you for far too long? Yes. Reprogram yourself with positive, beautiful affirmations that will be life altering, life changing for you? Yes. Will you commit to all of this, and anything further that will assist your healing and moving forward in your life and thriving? Yes.

So go on then. Go and be your authentic, beautiful self that's been hiding behind that wounded child in an adult body. I dare you. Go and be it. Yes, the narcissist/s in your life will hate and despise and loathe and envy you for it. Solely because you have what they don't. And it's an ongoing reminder to them of what they're not. And by now you know that they are always attempting to overcompensate due to their feelings of inadequacy.

Here's a thought: Leave them to stew. Leave them to fester. Leave them to get older and worse with it. It's not your problem. It never was. It never has been. Whilst they are weak, you are strong. A warrior.

My dear friend, are you ready? Are you excited? I know I am. I'm excited for you. Because your life of thriving is about to begin. It really is. The life of being the best that you can be? It's yours. You now have the tools. You now have the know how. You now know that all your vulnerabilities and insecurities is all that the narcissist has against you. Once they're gone, the attraction is gone. Nor can they affect you. Have nothing to say to them. Have nothing to prove to them. You're going to be comfortable in your own skin. So comfortable that they can't touch you. They can't affect you.

Deep breath in. Deep breath out. Deep breath in. Deep breath out. You have absolutely got this, my dear friend. How can I say this with such confidence? Because of the memory stick, of course. The memory stick that the narcissist/s in your life stomped on, tried to crush, and tried to remove. But, the truth is that it's been there all along. The memory stick has known all along that you actually want to love yourself. You just didn't know how. Now, my dear friend, go and shine. Go and thrive. That's the lot in life that you deserve. And you knew it the entire time.

ABOUT THE AUTHOR

Shayne N. Edson was affected personally by narcissistic abuse for approximately the first forty years of his life: not only by his NPD biological mother, but also by his NPD biological brother, malignant golden child biological sister, and even to some extent by his enabling codependent biological father. Resulting in his personally experiencing for many years complex PTSD, depression, and almost self annihilation.

Until he started looking for answers as to just what it was that he couldn't quite seem to put his finger on, yet unconsciously seemed to sense and know. Resulting in him not only healing from the negative impact of lifelong narcissistic abuse, but getting to a place where he was able to thrive on a daily basis. He doesn't simply talk the talk. He also walks the walk. He wants to help countless other victims to be able to do the same.

Shayne lives with his wife and teenage daughter in Canberra, the capital city of Australia.

Instagram: @shaynenedsonauthor
Twitter: @ShayneEdson
Website: shaynenedsonauthorcoach.wordpress.com

www.ingramcontent.com/pod-product-compliance
Lightning Source LLC
Chambersburg PA
CBHW051742250726
48659CB00001B/208